Professional Development Guide

Writing

Author

Marsha Roit

A Division of The McGraw·Hill Companies

Columbus, Ohio

Acknowledgments

This book would not have been possible without the efforts of the teachers and young authors at Cactus View Elementary School, Phoenix, AZ; North Ranch Elementary School, Scottsdale, AZ; Hamilton Elementary School, Chicago, IL; Glenmount Elementary School, Baltimore, MD; Red Oak Elementary School, Red Oak, NC; Hutchinson Elementary School, Greensburg, PA; Salazar Elementary School, Alice, TX; and Gardendale Elementary School, San Antonio, TX. Your contributions are truly appreciated. And, thank you to all the teachers and students over the years who have allowed me into their classrooms and shared so many of the ideas that are in this guide today.

Student writing samples have not been edited.

Photo Credits:

p. 5, ©Andy Sacks/Tony Stone Images; **p. 8,** ©Robert E. Daemmrich/Tony Stone Images; **p. 10,** ©Charles Gupton/The Stock Market; **p. 13,** ©Robert E. Daemmrich/ Tony Stone Images; **p. 18,** ©Michael Heron/The Stock Market; **p. 21,** ©Peter Cade/Tony Stone Images; **p. 36,** Image Bank; **p. 25,** ©Rob Lewine/The Stock Market; **p. 29,** ©Ian Shaw/Tony Stone Images; **p. 32,** ©Jeff M. Dunn/Stock Boston; **p. 33,** ©Peter Cade/Tony Stone Images; **p. 40,** ©Michael Krasowitz/FPG International

www.sra4kids.com

SRA/McGraw-Hill

A Division of The McGraw-Hill Companies

Send all inquiries to:
SRA/McGraw-Hill
8787 Orion Place
Columbus, Ohio 43240

Printed in the United States of America.

ISBN 0-07-571265-2

2 3 4 5 6 7 8 9 MAL 07 06 05 04 03 02

Table of Contents

Table of Contents

(continued)

Introduction to Writing

Writing is a complicated process. A writer fluently uses handwriting, spelling, vocabulary, grammar, usage, and mechanics skills with ideas to create readable text. A writer must know how to generate content, or ideas, and understand genre structures in order to effectively present ideas in writing. Familiarity with the structures of writing and different genres, audiences, and purposes is necessary to write appropriately, as well. The art of writing well also involves writer's craft, the ability to manipulate words and sentences for effect.

Many students never progress beyond producing a written text that duplicates their everyday speech patterns.

Mature writers, however, take composition beyond conversation. They understand the importance of audience and purpose for writing. They organize their thoughts, eliminating those that do not advance their main ideas, and elaborating on those that do, to ensure that their readers can follow a logical progression of ideas in an essay or story. Mature writers also know and can use the conventions of grammar, usage, spelling, and mechanics, enabling them to produce clear and precise texts. They proofread and edit to ensure that they have used conventions correctly, so their readers are not distracted by errors.

As strange as it may seem, the better a writer is, the harder he or she works at writing. It does not get easier with more expertise. It just gets better. The best writers are not the best because they are naturally talented. They are the best usually because they work the hardest. Good writers really do take more time than others in the planning and revising stages of the writing process. Poorer writers make writing look easy by writing without planning and typically build a composition sentence by sentence. They turn in their papers with no or only a few cursory corrections. A good writer cares about his or her message, the purpose for writing, and the audience.

The best writers are not the best because they are naturally talented. They are the best usually because they work the hardest.

Many adult writers believe that writing helps them think. For them, writing is a way of transforming knowledge into something more personal and/or useful. Most children have little experience with writing as a self-initiated, enjoyable activity that helps them think. The challenge in teaching writing is showing children how it is used by those who cherish it and by those who have made writing a profession.

An environment with an emphasis on writing provides a multifaceted context for the development of higher-order thinking. Students learn to plan, which allows them to work out ideas in their heads; to set goals, which promotes interest and the ability to monitor progress; and to revise content, which engages them in reworking and rethinking activities that elevate writing from a craft to a tool for discovery and knowledge transformation.

Elements of Writing

The Writing Process

Writers spend time thinking about and planning their topics. They choose their own topics from a number of sources, including their interests—what they care about, dream about, or have experienced—and what they have yet to learn. They also know how to become personally invested in an assigned topic. Writers consider their audience, let their ideas grow in their minds, and develop and conduct research, if necessary, before they ever begin writing.

- Writers draft or put their ideas into words. They get their ideas down on paper, often in a rough form.
- Writers revise and revisit their work. They take another look to see if it makes sense and to see if it says what they want it to say. They check to be sure the meaning is clear for the reader.
- Writers edit their work. Good writers recognize the importance of writing conventions—grammar, mechanics, and spelling—that allow the reader to understand and enjoy published works.
- Writers go public. They publish their work in books, newspapers, magazines, anthologies, and so on.

Writing is a recursive process: authors move back and forth through writing activities—from planning to drafting to revising and back—to create their final pieces.

Writing is a recursive process: authors move back and forth through writing activities—from planning to drafting to revising and back—to create their final pieces. It is a process of thinking, experimenting, and evaluating.

All writers need feedback throughout the writing process. They need reactions to ideas, drafts, and revisions before it is too late to make changes.

Writing Genres and Forms of Writing

There are several different genres students are typically asked to write. These usually include many creative stories and a few reports. The only narrative writing most adults do, however, might be summaries of meetings. The bulk of adult writing consists of writing reports, letters, analyses, memos, and proposals. College students as well typically write research reports or critiques. A literate student needs to be able to choose and write in appropriate genres. These may include:

- **Narrative writing** is story writing, that has a beginning, middle, and end. It includes realistic fiction, historical fiction, biography, science fiction, fantasy, folktale, myth, and legend.
- **Expository writing** is informational writing. It includes research reports, summary, analysis essay, and explanation of a process.
- **Descriptive writing** is observational writing that includes details. It includes observation reports and descriptive paragraphs that may be part of narrative or expository writing.
- **Poetry writing** involves paying particular attention to word choice and rhythm. Poetry may be free form, rhyming, or a variety of other forms.
- **Personal writing** is functional writing to help record ideas, thoughts, or feelings or to communicate with others. It includes e-mail, journals, lists, and messages.
- **Persuasive writing** involves the development of a persuasive argument. It includes persuasive essays, advertisements, posters, editorials, and letters to the editor.

Each genre has its own structure. For example:

- A **personal narrative** is probably best ordered as a straightforward chronological retelling of events. Dialogue may help to tell the story.
- An **explanation of a process** should be told in a step-by-step order. The draft should include as much information as possible; each step must be clear.
- A **persuasive** piece appeals to feelings and logic. It requires facts as well as expert opinions.
- The order of details in a **descriptive** piece must be easy to follow—from left to right, top to bottom, or whatever order makes sense.
- A **fictional story** must include details describing characters, setting, and the characters' actions. Dialogue and suspense also help to tell the story.

Structures of writing should be taught within the context of the Writing Process rather than in isolation, so that students integrate their practice of writing structures as they develop different writing genres.

Structures of Writing

Structures of writing involve the effective development of sentences, paragraphs, and compositions. Structures of writing should be taught within the context of the Writing Process rather than in isolation, so that students integrate their practice of writing structures as they develop different writing genres.

Writer's Craft

Writer's craft involves the elements a writer uses to add drama, suspense, or surprise to a written work. These elements may include foreshadowing, use of figurative language, dialogue, enhancement of setting, or use of description to affect the mood and tone. Writer's craft may also include adding description, detail, and evidence to nonfictional writing. Literature is comprised of excellent models of writer's craft that can be then taught and practiced within the context of the Writing Process Strategies.

Writing Traits

Writing traits are those elements and qualities in a composition that enhance the effectiveness of the writing. These include:

- **Ideas/Content.** Not only the quality of the idea, but the development, support, and focus of the idea make a strong composition.
- **Organization.** In quality writing, the organization develops the central idea. The order and structure move the reader through the text easily. The beginning grabs the reader's attention and the conclusion adds impact.
- **Voice.** Voice is the overall tone of a piece of writing. Good writers choose a voice appropriate for the topic, purpose, and audience. As students develop writing skills, a unique style begins to emerge. The writing is expressive, engaging, or sincere, demonstrating a strong commitment to the topic.
- **Word Choice.** In quality writing words convey the intended message in an interesting, precise, and natural way appropriate to audience and purpose.
- **Sentence Fluency.** Sentence fluency enhances the flow and rhythm of a composition. In good writing sentence patterns are somewhat varied, contributing to ease in oral reading.
- **Conventions.** Good writers demonstrate consistent use and awareness of English language conventions.
- **Presentation.** A quality piece of writing includes an impressive presentation with attention to format, style, illustration, and clarity.

Grammar, Usage, and Mechanics for Writing

The Study of English Conventions

Over the years the study of grammar, usage, and mechanics has gone in and out of favor. In the past century much research has been done to demonstrate the effectiveness of traditional types of instruction in the conventions of English. Experience and research have shown that learning grammatical terms and completing grammar exercises have little effect on the student's practical application of these skills in the context of speaking or writing. These skills, in and of themselves, do not play a significant role in the way students use language to generate and express their ideas, particularly during the prewriting and drafting phases of the writing process. In fact, emphasis on correct conventions has been shown to have a damaging effect when it is the sole focus of writing instruction. If students are evaluated only on the proper use of spelling, grammar, and punctuation, they tend to write fewer and less complex sentences.

Knowledge of English conventions is, however, vitally important in the editing and proofreading phases of the writing process. A paper riddled with mistakes in grammar, usage, or mechanics is quickly discounted. Many immature writers never revise or edit. They finish the last sentence and turn their papers in to the teacher. Mature writers employ their knowledge of English language conventions in the editing phase to refine and polish their ideas.

Mature writers employ their knowledge of English language conventions in the editing phase to refine and polish their ideas.

The study of grammar, usage, and mechanics is important for two reasons:

1. Educated people need to know and understand the structure of their language, which in large part defines their culture.
2. Knowledge of grammar gives teachers and students a common vocabulary for talking about language and makes discussions of writing tasks more efficient and clear.

The key issue in learning grammar, usage, and mechanics is how to teach it. On the one hand, teaching these skills in isolation from writing has been shown to be ineffective and even detrimental if too much emphasis is placed on them. On the other hand, not teaching these skills and having students write without concern for conventions is equally ineffective. The answer is to teach the skills in a context that allows students to directly apply them in a reading or writing activity. Students should be taught conventions, such as punctuation or subject/verb agreement so that they can use them with enough fluency that they do not belabor sentence construction to the detriment of their ideas as they draft. They should then be taught to proofread for those conventions. As they learn to apply their knowledge of conventions during the final stages of the writing process, they will begin to see that correcting errors is an editorial, rather than a composing skill.

Grammar is the sound, structure, and meaning system of language. People who speak the same language are able to communicate because they intuitively know the grammar system of that language, or the rules of making meaning. All languages have grammar, and yet each language has its own grammar.

Traditional grammar study usually involves two areas:

- **Parts of speech** (nouns, verbs, adjectives, adverbs, pronouns, infinitives, conjunctions) are typically considered the content of grammar. The parts of speech involve the form of English words.
- **Sentence structure** (subjects, predicates, objects, clauses, phrases) is also included in grammar study. Sentence structure involves the function of English.

Mechanics involves the conventions of punctuation and capitalization. Punctuation helps readers understand writers' messages. In speech, students can produce sentences as easily and unconsciously as they can walk. In writing, however, punctuation identifies what is and what is not a sentence.

In English there are about twelve punctuation marks (period, comma, quotation marks, question mark, exclamation point, colon, semicolon, hyphen, ellipsis, parentheses, brackets, dash). Most immature writers use only three: period, comma, and question mark. The experienced writer or poet with command of punctuation adds both flexibility and meaning to his or her sentences through the use of punctuation.

Usage Language varies over time, across national and geographical boundaries, by gender, across age groups, and by socioeconomic status. When the variation occurs within a given language, the different versions of the same language are called dialects. Every language has a prestige dialect associated with education and financial success. In the United States, this dialect is known as Standard English and is the language of school and business.

Usage involves the word choices people make when speaking certain dialects. Word choices that are perfectly acceptable in conversation among friends may be unacceptable in writing. Usage is often the most obvious indicator of the difference between conversation and composition. Errors in word usage can make a writer seem ignorant and thus jeopardize his or her credibility, no matter how valid or important his or her overall message might be. If the dialect children have learned is not the formal language of school settings or if it is not English, children must master another dialect or language in order to write Standard English.

If the dialect children have learned is not the formal language of school settings or if it is not English, children must master another dialect or language in order to write Standard English.

In a balanced literacy program, English Language Conventions are taught in two ways. First, the skills are presented in a logical sequence. A skill is introduced with appropriate models and then practiced in reading and writing on subsequent days to ensure that skills are not taught in isolation. Second, short lessons are tailored to specific skills that support a particular form of writing or that reinforce a skill students may be having difficulty implementing. With practice, students should be able to apply their knowledge of conventions to any writing they do.

Spelling and Writing

Spelling is a fundamental skill in written communication. Although a writer may have wonderful ideas, he or she may find it difficult to communicate those ideas without spelling skills. Learning to spell requires much exposure to text and writing, and for many it requires a methodical presentation of English spelling patterns. Just as the goal of phonics instruction is to enable students to read fluently, the goal of spelling instruction is to enable students to write fluently so they can concentrate on their ideas rather than their spelling.

The most important finding in spelling research in the past thirty years is that students learn to spell in a predictable developmental sequence, much as they learn to read.

The most important finding in spelling research in the past thirty years is that students learn to spell in a predictable developmental sequence, much as they learn to read. It appears to take the average child from three to six years to progress through the developmental stages and emerge as a fairly competent, mature speller.

Beginnings of Writing

Young children come to school knowing a lot about writing. Just watch any young child with a crayon and paper making lines and squiggles and pictures. Upon completion the youngster proudly shares the piece by telling a story. This emerging writer knows that writing communicates and that authors use marks (letters) and pictures to share thoughts and ideas. Our roles as teachers of young writers are to coach, encourage, and help children move toward conventional writing.

Writing is developmental. Often during the early stages, we are transcribers as children draw, then dictate, their stories to us. As children learn about our alphabet and begin connecting letters and sounds, they should be prompted to do their own writing, using letters and incomplete spelling. Each child's progress is going to be unique. Some may skip a stage or phase; some may seem to spend forever doing the same thing; and some may continue to use incomplete spelling even into second grade.

Young authors in kindergarten and first grade progress through a series of stages or phases, which are all precursors to more conventional, or standard, writing.

Early Writing Observations

- Scribble writing—lines and scribbles about which the writer tells a story
- Drawing stories (pictures) and telling about them
- Random letters
- Randomly using uppercase and lowercase letters and numbers
- Using groups of letters with spaces in between
- Copying words and sentences from books and labels in the classroom
- Using beginning and ending consonants and single letters to labels parts of pictures or to write sentences

- Attempting to spell. In addition to beginning and ending sounds, vowels are added and the words can be read (with some deciphering) by adults.
- Using conventional spellings for high-frequency words

Teaching Strategies for Writing

The teacher's role in writing instruction is critical. Practice makes permanent, not perfect. If young writers write a lot, badly, their bad writing becomes permanent. People do not become better writers by writing a lot. They become better writers by writing *well* a lot. Teachers teach them how to do it. Merely promoting writing deludes children into believing that enthusiasm is sufficient in learning to write. It is not sufficient and it might not even be necessary. Certain teaching strategies have been shown to be particularly effective in teaching writing.

Teacher Modeling Students understand and learn best when they have good models to follow. Models for the different forms of writing appear in literature. Teachers or other students must provide the models for the writing process, as well. Teachers can also model the writing process for students every time they write.

Writing Frequency In many classrooms students write fewer than four compositions in a year. This gives them little practice writing and promotes a fear of writing. Students should be writing frequently to develop writing fluency. To simplify the assessment of writing, rubrics can be established beforehand so that each composition is evaluated on only a few traits.

Genre The different genres and forms of writing should be explicitly described and modeled. Too much elementary school writing is creative story writing. Yet story writing does not prepare students to ask and answer questions, write coherent directions, or send a thank you note. Exploring different genres and their structures gives students experience and practice writing a variety of different forms.

Feedback The most effective writing instruction is the feedback good teachers give to individual student work. Unfortunately many teachers simply mark errors in spelling, grammar, usage, and mechanics and do not comment on the traits of writing: ideas, organization, voice, and so on. Conference questions and assessment should provide questions that teachers can consider to offer constructive and meaningful feedback to students.

> ***The most effective writing instruction is the feedback good teachers give to individual student work.***

Clear Assignments A well-written assignment makes clear to students what they are supposed to do, how they are supposed to do it, who the students are writing for, and what constitutes a successful composition. When students have this information, they can plan, organize, and produce more effective work.

Instruction Students need specific examples, instruction, and practice with different forms of writing and on different phases of the writing process. With instruction, modeling, practice, and feedback, students will see that some people are not "just born with a talent for writing."

Using a Word Processor Many students enjoy drafting on a computer more than drafting on paper. Once they have mastered the keyboard they may find it easier to think as they write. Their first attempts look less sloppy, and they are often more willing to make changes and experiment as they draft. They are more likely to rearrange, add, or delete text if they know they don't have to recopy the entire composition. They will certainly find it neater to use the delete key of a word processor than to correct their mistakes by erasing or crossing out. In addition, word processing tools such as spell and grammar checkers, and multimedia presentation features add to the finished product.

Writing Process Strategies

Prewriting

Prewriting is that phase of the writing process when students think through an idea they want to write about. To improve their writing, students should think about their ideas, discuss them, and plan how they want readers to respond. It is important for students to take time before writing to plan ahead so that they can proceed from one phase of the writing process to another without spending unnecessary time making decisions that should have been made earlier. Prewriting is the most time-consuming phase of the writing process, but it may be the most important.

Good Student Writers:

- Listen to advice about time requirements and plan time accordingly.
- Spend time choosing, thinking about, and planning the topic.
- Spend time narrowing the topic.
- Determine the purpose for writing.
- Consider the audience and what readers already know about the topic.
- Conduct research, if necessary, before writing.
- Get information from a lot of different sources.
- Use models for different types of writing, but develop individual plans.

- Organize the resource information.
- Make a plan for writing that shows how the ideas will be organized.
- Elaborate on a plan and evaluate and alter ideas as writing proceeds.

Writing Ideas

Students can make notes of writing ideas at any time, with a special time being set aside following the discussion of each reading selection. The writing ideas students get from a discussion might be concerned with the topic of the selection they just read or with an aspect of the author's style. You should keep such a list of writing ideas also, and think aloud occasionally as you make writing-idea notes.

The class can brainstorm about where to get ideas for writing (books, personal experiences, family, places children have gone, things they want to learn more about, things they like to do, and so on). Then a list of ideas can be started and kept prominently displayed in the classroom. Teacher modeling of writing inspiration and getting ideas is valuable.

Professional writers keep journals and/or notebooks of writing ideas. Writers put down all kinds of ideas—some good, some not so good—because they never know when these ideas will be useful. For example, a writer might jot down a few lines of dialogue overheard on a bus, a brief description of a tree, or a line from a popular song. The writer may never use these bits in a story. Or, he or she may find months later that this is perfect for a character being developed in a story.

Prewriting Decisions

Students must make many decisions during the prewriting phase of the writing process. Most students can benefit from talking with a partner or a small group of classmates about these decisions. They may want to discuss some of the following points.

- **Genre** of each writing piece. Having decided to use a writing idea such as "a misunderstanding on the first day of school," the student must decide how to use it—for example, as a personal narrative, a realistic fiction story, a poem, a fantasy story, a play, a letter, or whatever.
- **Audience** Although students' writing pieces will be shared with classmates and with you, some may ultimately be intended for other audiences. For example, a student might write a letter to a congressperson or write an article to adult readers in his or her community.
- **Writing Purpose** Each student should write a sentence that tells the purpose of the piece he or she plans to write. The purpose statement should name the intended audience and the effect the writer hopes to have on that audience. For example, a writer may want to describe her first day in school. The intended audience is kindergarten students, and she intends her story to be humorous. Her purpose statement would read, "I want to write a funny story for little students about my first day in kindergarten."
- **Planning** Some writers may find it helpful to brainstorm with a partner or small group to list words and phrases they might use in a piece of writing. Sometimes this list can be organized into webs of related ideas or details. This kind of prewriting activity might be particularly useful for planning a descriptive piece. For planning a comparison/ contrast piece, a writer might use another kind of visual organizer, such as a Venn diagram. Students planning fiction pieces might use a story map or plot-line diagram.

Drafting

During the drafting phase of the writing process students shape their planning notes into main ideas and details. They devote their time and effort to getting words down on paper. Whether students are drafting on scrap paper or on computer screens, your role is to encourage each writer to "get it all down." You must also provide a suitable writing environment with the expectation that there will be revisions to the draft and to the original plan.

Students should try to get their ideas down on paper as quickly and as completely as possible. As they turn their notes into sentences and paragraphs, students should keep in mind their intended audience and their reasons for writing each particular piece.

Allow adequate time for drafting. Students may not all work at the same pace. Some students may work on one part of a piece at a time, revising the first part before they draft the second. Others may write the whole piece in one sitting. In a classroom full of drafters, then, some students will be thinking, some muttering to themselves, some writing, and some reading what they have written. Keep in mind that some students will not be able to concentrate on their writing for more than 15 to 20 minutes. However, allow more time for those who need it.

Remind students not to be limited by their notes as they write their drafts. Students will find that the very act of writing can cause them to think in new ways. They will think of new connections between ideas and of new details to add that will develop their ideas. Some of them may even decide to change their topics. This is all part of the excitement of shaping ideas into sentences.

Modeling Drafting

Using a board, a large chart, or an overhead transparency, teachers can model drafting for the students by turning their own prewriting

notes into sentences and paragraphs. Teachers should think aloud as they put their ideas into words, working quickly. Teachers can demonstrate the following as they model.

- Use your plan and your notes from research to add details.
- Write on every other line so that you will have room to make revisions.
- Write on only one side of a page so that when you revise you can see all of your draft at once.
- Leave a blank space when you have difficulty thinking of the best word.
- Put parentheses around words that should be replaced.
- Use abbreviations and invented spellings.
- Cross out words or sentences or draw arrows to indicate that they should be moved to a different place.
- Use a caret to insert new words.
- Think aloud.
- Indicate that an idea is not complete and will need more detail or research.
- Make adjustments in the plan or outline when it isn't working.
- As you draft, keep in mind your purpose for writing this piece and your intended audience.

Good Student Writers:

- Express all of their ideas in the first draft.
- Stop and think about what is being written while drafting.
- Evaluate and alter ideas while drafting.
- Change or elaborate on original plans while drafting.
- Discover that they need more information about certain parts of their writing.
- Learn a lot more about the topic while drafting.

Tips

Sometimes the hardest part of drafting is getting the first sentence down on paper. It may help a student who feels stuck even before she or he starts writing to begin a story in the middle or to write the word "Draft" in big letters at the top of the paper.

If a student feels stuck during drafting, he or she may need to go back and try a different prewriting technique.

After an initial fifteen or twenty minutes of imposed silence, some students may work better and come up with more ideas if they share as they write.

You may find that it is difficult to get students to "loosen up" as they draft. Remember, most students have been encouraged to be neat and to erase mistakes when they write. It may help to share some of your own drafts with students.

Revising

The purpose of revising is to make sure that a piece of writing expresses the writer's ideas clearly and completely. It has been said that there is no good writing, just good rewriting. A major distinction between good writers and poor writers is the amount of time and effort they put into revision. Poor writers look for spelling and grammatical errors if they do read their work.

Revising is a difficult concept for students to understand, let alone do. It often is ignored, misunderstood, or left to the teacher to do before handing back the corrected copies. Revising involves critical thinking. Writers revise by stepping back and reexamining their own work. The revision process allows authors to evaluate the clarity of content and ideas in their work. Besides considering the ideas in a piece of writing, a writer also considers whether the piece fulfills the requirements of its genre and concentrates on paragraphs, sentences, and words.

The revision process allows authors to evaluate the clarity of content and ideas in their work.

Writers may revise at any time in the writing process. Some authors draft and revise simultaneously; others prefer to complete a draft and then revise.

A good time to introduce the concept of revising is during writing conferences by asking students to clarify or extend a sentence. Initially, help students by asking them to expand on where something happened, when it happened, why it happened, or how it happened. One common reason students don't revise is that they think this means recopying everything. Revising can be done without recopying.

Initially authors should be encouraged to take responsibility for two or three of these revision techniques and to attempt more as they learn new skills. Remember, revising will look different for different children. Emergent writers may revise pictures by adding details or labels. As they start more conventional writing, young authors usually will revise by adding information to the ends of their stories. As their understanding grows, they will begin revising by inserting information as they elaborate on their ideas.

Modeling Revising

Students understand and learn best when they have good models to follow. Teachers can use a rough draft and model revising in this way:

1. Read through the entire composition quickly, thinking aloud and taking quick notes about things to change. This allows you to get a sense of the entire work before trying to work on details. It helps you see if things have to be moved or if logic is faulty. For example,
   - *This doesn't make sense.*
   - *I forgot to finish this sentence.*
   - *I don't have a very good beginning.*
   - *This paragraph makes a better ending than the one I have.*
2. Read through a second time and address specifics. Think aloud. For example,
   - *I think I should move this to the end.*
   - *I need a better word here.*
   - *This is good. I'll keep it as it is.*
   - *I should say more about this. I'll add more details to describe this.*
   - *Now this idea doesn't fit. I'll cross it out.*
3. Demonstrate some shortcuts for revising. Make arrows to show how to move words or sentences.
4. Elicit and discuss any suggestions from the students for further revisions. Make additional changes, if necessary, based on their suggestions. Remind students that during the revision phase of the writing process, it is important to get feedback from others.
5. Explain that you may revise this draft more than once—*writing is a recursive process.*
   - **About a narrative:**
     ✓ *Does my first sentence get my readers' attention?*
     ✓ *Are events in the story told in an order that makes sense?*
     ✓ *Have I included dialogue to help move the story along?*
     ✓ *Does the story have a clear focus?*
   - **About a description:**
     ✓ *Have I used details that appeal to the senses?*
   - **About a comparison/contrast piece:**
     ✓ *Have I written a separate paragraph for each subject discussed?*
   - **About an explanation:**
     ✓ *Will readers understand what I am saying?*
     ✓ *Are the steps of the explanation in a clear order?*
     ✓ *Have I made effective use of signal words?*
     ✓ *Have I included enough information?*
   - **About fiction:**
     ✓ *Have I described my characters and setting?*
     ✓ *Does the plot include a problem, build to a climax, and then describe the resolution of the problem?*
   - **About persuasive writing:**
     ✓ *Have I made my position clear?*
     ✓ *Does my evidence support my position?*
     ✓ *Have I used opinions as well as facts, and have I said whose opinions I used?*
     ✓ *Have I directed my writing to my audience?*
6. Help students understand the value of asking questions such as the following as they revise.
   - **About each paragraph:**
     ✓ *Does each sentence belong in it?*
     ✓ *Does each sentence connect smoothly with the next?*
     ✓ *Does each sentence say something about the main idea?*
   - **About each sentence:**
     ✓ *Do the sentences read smoothly?*
     ✓ *Have I combined sentences that were too short?*
     ✓ *Have I broken sentences that were too long into two shorter sentences?*
     ✓ *Have I varied the beginnings of the sentences?*

- **About the words:**
  ✓ *Have I changed words that were repeated too often?*
  ✓ *Do transition words connect ideas?*

Good Student Writers:

- Look back and evaluate what has been written.
- Consider audience, purpose, and form.
- Read the draft repeatedly from a reader's perspective.
- Identify problems with focus, giving enough information, clarity, and order.
- Think of solutions to problems and understand when solutions will and will not work.
- Recognize when and how the text needs to be reorganized.
- Eliminate sentences or paragraphs that don't fit the main idea.
- Identify ideas that need elaboration.
- Do more research if needed to support or add ideas.
- Identify and eliminate unnecessary details.
- Combine or extend sentences using how, when, where, and why questions.
- Elaborate, using dialogue, narrative techniques, and descriptive language.
- Check to see if sentences and paragraphs are in a logical order.
- Ask for feedback from peer and teacher conferences.
- Take advantage of classroom and outside resources.
- Check the accuracy of facts and details.
- Give credit for any ideas from other people or sources.
- Present and support personal points of view and ideas.

Tips

- Use the student Writing Folder to review student progress. Check first drafts against revised versions to see how each student is able to apply revision strategies.
- If a student doesn't see anything that needs to be changed or doesn't want to change anything, get him or her to do something to the paper—number the details in a description or the steps in a process, circle exact words, underline the best parts of the paper. Once a paper is marked, the student may not be so reluctant to change it.
- One reason many students do not like to revise is that they think they must recopy everything. This is not always necessary. Sometimes writers can cut and paste sections that they want to move. Or they can use carets and deletion marks to show additions to and subtractions from a piece.
- Give an especially reluctant student a deadline by which she or he must revise a piece or lose the chance to publish it.
- Students will hopefully be writing in other classes and on a variety of topics. Revision techniques can be used to improve writing in any curricular area. Stress to students the importance of focusing on their intended audience as they revise.

Editing/Proofreading

After a piece of writing has been revised for content and style, students must read it carefully line by line to make sure that it contains no errors. This activity, the fourth phase of the writing process, is called editing or proofreading and is a critical step that must occur before a piece of writing can be published. Students can begin proofreading a piece when they feel that it has been sufficiently revised.

Writing that is free of grammatical, spelling, and technical mistakes is clearer and easier for readers to understand. By proofreading their pieces, students will also notice which errors they make repeatedly and will learn not to make them in the future. In editing, the writer concentrates on cleaning up the surface errors after meaning has been developed and ideas are clarified. This is done so the reader can focus on understanding and enjoying a story. Students should apply the same editing skills to any writing they do.

Students should be expected to proofread at a level appropriate to their grade. Young authors should not be held responsible for skills they have not yet learned. Older students will be able to check for a greater variety of errors than younger students and should be expected to take greater responsibility for their proofreading. Older students will have mastered many more grammatical, mechanical, usage, and spelling skills and can be expected to perform accordingly. When you spot an error related to a skill beyond a student's level, make clear to the student that you do not expect her or him to be responsible for the mistake, but do explain that the error still needs to be corrected. The following suggestions may be useful as you introduce proofreading to the students and help them develop their proofreading skills.

- **Spelling List** Encourage students to keep a list of frequently misspelled words. If a student notes the same type of mistakes over and over in writing, suggest that the student review the rules. Then praise the student when the problem has been resolved.
- **Colored Pencil** Suggest that students use a colored pencil to mark errors so they can read corrections easily.
- **Proofreading Tips** If some students find the proofreading process intimidating, suggest that they read their work several times and check for only a few types of errors each time. If children are having difficulty spotting errors in sentence structure, suggest that they read the paragraph backward, last sentence to first. This process may help students look at each sentence individually.
- **Student Ownership** Be careful not to take ownership of the writing away from the students. Students always must understand that the pieces are theirs. Try to resist the temptation to rewrite students' work. The student's voice, with his or her own vocabulary, should come through in the piece.
- **Revising** If a significant error is noticed at the proofreading stage, suggest that the student revise the piece once more.
- **Letting Go** Some students have trouble letting go of a piece; that is, they cannot stop revising and proofreading. If this is a problem, encourage the students to publish. Often affirmation and encouragement are all a student needs to build enough confidence to stop revising. If older students have this problem, set a publication deadline. Tell them that professional writers and editors work with such deadlines. Teachers should use their own judgment to determine how flexible the deadline is in each case.
- **Proofreading Marks** Students should use standard proofreading marks to indicate the changes they wish to make. Explain to

students that these marks are a kind of code used to show which alterations to make without a long explanation. Students may also be interested to know that professional writers, editors, and proofreaders use these same marks. You may want to review these marks one by one, illustrating on the board how to use them. For example, they may insert a word or a phrase by using a caret (^). If students wish to insert more text than will fit above the line, they may write in the margin or attach another sheet of paper. It may be a good idea, when such extensive corrections are made, for students to proofread their final copy carefully to make sure they have included all their alterations.

- **Teacher Modeling** Teachers can model good proofreading skills for the students by proofreading a piece of their own writing. Be sure to include specific errors (misspelled words, incorrect capitalization, repeated words, incorrect paragraph indentation, and so on) so that all the proofreading marks are used.
- **Peer Input** Input from peers is an effective way to strengthen proofreading skills. After a student has proofread a piece of writing, suggest that he or she ask a classmate to proofread it again. The classmate should use a different colored pen or pencil to mark any new changes. After each paper has been returned, remind the students to review the changes marked by their classmate to make sure they want to make these changes. Students who are proofreading a classmate's paper should be encouraged to notice strengths as well as errors in a piece.
- **Sentence Lifting** is a very effective method of showing students how to proofread their own work. Because students are working on their own sentences, they will be more inclined to both pay attention to what is going on and better understand the corrections that are made.
  - Choose several pieces of student writing and look for common errors.
  - On an overhead, write several sentences. Include at least one sentence that has no errors.
  - Tell students that you are going to concentrate on one type of error at a time. For example, first you will concentrate on spelling.
  - Ask students to read the first sentence and point out any words they feel are spelled incorrectly. Do not erase errors. Cross them out and write the correctly spelled word above the crossed-out word.
  - Next move to a different type of error. Ask students to check for capitalization and punctuation.
  - Continue in this way, correcting errors as you go through the sample sentences.
- **Using Word Processing Software** If the students are using a word processing program to write their pieces, they may wish to run a spell check on their document. Caution them, however, that even the most sophisticated software cannot catch every spelling error. The software will not catch misuse of homophones and other words if the misused words appear in the software's dictionary. For example, if a student types *form* instead of *from*, the software will not register a mistake because *form* is also a word. Circulate as students are proofreading on their own or in pairs. The following are questions to consider as you evaluate students' proofreading:
  - Are students able to check references when they are unsure of a spelling or usage?

- Are students criticizing each other's work constructively?
- Does a student no longer omit end punctuation because he or she noticed this error repeatedly during proofreading?
- Note students who are having difficulty. You may wish to address these difficulties during individual conferences.

Proofreading Checklist

Have students use a proofreading checklist similar to the one shown here to help them remember the steps for effective proofreading.

- ☑ Read each sentence.
- ☑ Does each sentence begin with a capital letter and end with correct punctuation?
- ☑ Do you notice any fragments or run-on sentences?
- ☑ Are words missing from the sentence?
- ☑ Is any punctuation or capitalization missing from within the sentence?
- ☑ Do you notice any incorrect grammar or incorrect word usage in the sentence?
- ☑ Do you notice any misspelled words?
- ☑ Are the paragraphs indented?

Good Student Writers:

- Edit the work to allow the reader to understand and enjoy the work.
- Correct most errors in English language conventions.
- Use resources or seek assistance to address any uncertainties in English language conventions.

Publishing

Publishing is the process of bringing private writing to the reading public. The purpose of writing is to communicate. Unless students are writing in a journal, they will want to present their writing to the public. Such sharing helps students to learn about themselves and others, provides an opportunity for them to take pride in their hard work, and thus motivates them to further writing.

Publishing their work helps motivate students to improve such skills as spelling, grammar, and handwriting.

Publishing their work helps motivate students to improve such skills as spelling, grammar, and handwriting. Publishing can be as simple as displaying papers on a bulletin board or as elaborate as creating a class newspaper. Publishing will not—indeed should not—always require large blocks of class time. Students will wish to spend more time elaborately presenting their favorite pieces and less time on other works. If students take an inordinate amount of time to publish their work, you may want to coach them on how to speed up the process.

Good Student Writers:

- Present the work in a way that makes it easy to read and understand.
- Consider format, style, illustration, as well as clarity in the presentation of the work.
- Show pride in the finished work.

Preparing the Final Copy

When students feel that they have thoroughly proofread their pieces, they should copy the work onto another sheet of paper using their best handwriting, or type the work on a computer or typewriter. They should then check this copy against the proofread copy to make sure that they made all the changes correctly and did not introduce any new errors. You may need to proofread and correct students' papers one final time before publishing to make sure that they have caught all errors.

Publishing Choices

In publishing, students need to decide

- how to prepare the piece for publication.
- what form the published work should take.
- whether to illustrate their writing with photographs, drawings, or charts with captions, as necessary.
- where to place text in relation to any art they are using.

Students should be aware that the way they present their ideas, which includes the package the ideas come in, greatly influences the effectiveness of their communication.

If a student is publishing a fairy tale or a story intended for younger children, she or he may wish to read the story aloud to a class of younger students. You could establish that during the last 15 minutes of the school day, students who have recently finished stories or other appropriate pieces could read their work to other classes.

If a student is publishing an article on a subject that might interest people in the school or community, suggest that he or she think about submitting the article to a school or community newspaper or magazine.

If a student is publishing something related to the explorable concepts of a unit in the student anthology, suggest that she or he consider displaying the piece on the Concept/Question Board.

Remind students that they will need to make decisions about the following elements:

- size and shape of finished product
- hard or soft cover (if book)
- placement of and captions for art
- arrangement of text (especially for poetry)
- size and style of type or writing

Students also must decide whether they wish to include a dedication, a table of contents

(useful in a long, nonfiction piece), a glossary (for technical pieces), a bibliography (for research papers), an author biography (for back cover of book), or a summary (for back cover of book).

If several students have written related pieces and are unsure of how to publish, they may wish to work together to create a newspaper or an anthology. A desktop-publishing program designed for children is especially useful in designing and laying out a newspaper. Encourage students to publish at least one piece as a group during the year.

Getting Creative

Encourage students to use their imaginations when publishing. Let them know that they may try many feasible methods of presenting their material. Some students may need some guidance and suggestions for how to publish and how best to use the supplies in the Publishing Center.

One traditional way to publish is to make a book. Suggest the following ways to make a book.

- A simple book is made by stapling together the pages, including the front and back covers, on the left side.
- An accordion book is made by pleating a long piece of paper.

- A plank book is made by binding together heavy pages of cardboard or thin wood with a string looped through holes in the pages.

Many methods are available to students for publishing their work besides making a book. Encourage the children to try new ways to present their work, especially if students always publish in the same two or three ways. Remind them that a creative or unusual presentation helps to capture and hold an audience's attention. Students might

- present their piece as a pamphlet.
- perform a play or puppet show for the class.
- participate in a writing contest.
- submit an article or letter to the editor of a magazine or newspaper.
- read a piece to music.
- perform a dance to a reading of a piece of writing.
- display writing on a bulletin board inside or outside the classroom.
- present a reading on videotape or audiotape.
- present the piece in a letter to a friend, relative, or pen pal.
- give a speech or dramatic reading for the class.
- make a comic book.
- present a mock radio or TV interview.
- include a piece in an anthology.
- include a piece in a class newspaper.

Students also can be creative with the design for their publication. In order to make their published work more interesting, students might

- make a very large or very small book.
- make a book in an unusual shape, such as a triangle or a circle.
- arrange text unusually, such as in a circle or at the very top or bottom of the page.

The following devices can be particularly appropriate for poetry.

- Paste pages on a cylindrical (such as a coffee can) or cubical (such as a small box) container. This technique allows students to place items related to the piece inside the container.
- Write passages in all capital or all small letters to change emphasis.
- Write in different colored ink to change emphasis.

Publishing Center

The Publishing Center in the classroom is established to help students publish their writing. It is stocked with materials for creating finished publications. Make sure the students understand what materials are available to them and how they should be used. Instruct them to work quietly in the center. You may want to post a sign-up sheet if you notice many students competing for supplies. Supplies could include

- lined and unlined paper in several colors and sizes.
- writing tools such as pens, pencils, colored pencils, markers, and crayons.
- supplies for lettering such as stencils, cutout letters, and models of calligraphy or other fancy alphabets.
- art supplies such as tracing paper, books of clip art, water-based paints, paintbrushes, sponges, colored construction paper, tissue paper, magazines for clipping pictures, and rubber stamps and ink pads.
- materials for book covers such as cardboard, posterboard, wallpaper or fabric (out-of-date sample books and roll ends are often available free), and wrapping paper.
- binding materials such as yarn, string, and dental floss.

- other supplies such as scissors, stapler, ruler, three-ring punch, paste or glue, clear adhesive tape, and correction fluid.
- a typewriter or a computer and printer.

Computers and Publishing

Many classrooms now include computers capable of word processing and desktop publishing. If such equipment is accessible, your students can produce a professional looking book or newspaper quite easily. Younger students may need extra help typing and using the software. Instruct them in how to use the equipment as needed. If a few children have trouble, ask other classmates to help or, if appropriate, have an older student come in to tutor them. If available, teachers may wish to use a word processing program designed specifically for children. Post a sign-up sheet for the computer if many children want to use this publishing method.

The Finished Product

When students are ready with their publications, check them over quickly to make sure there are no glaring errors before they present them to the public. Remember, this is student work and changes should not be made unless a serious problem is found.

Encourage students to put published works in the classroom library so that others can read them and use them as a reference. They can make their book more like a library book by making a checkout card for the book and placing it in an envelope pasted in the front or back of their book.

Students will want to take their work home to share with families. Finished publications provide tangible proof of student progress and are thus an important part of the home/school connection.

Students should select their best work for their assessment portfolio. If a chosen piece is in the library or at home, they can place a photocopy or a note in the portfolio indicating where the original is. Students might want to keep lists of all their published works in their portfolios.

Tips

- It is important to offer students an opportunity to present and celebrate their published work. Schedule class time for student performances and presentations as needed. If several students are ready at once, you may wish to invite other classes or family members to a group presentation. You could help the children prepare a program for the event.

- Displays inside and outside the classroom are useful ways for students to present their work. An exhibit in a common school area, such as the library or lobby, makes it possible for students to share their work with a larger audience. Public libraries, community centers, town halls, and banks are often interested in displaying work from the community's children.
- To further recognize student achievement, you may wish to select a "Writer of the Week." Items for display might include a list of the writer's published works, his or her photograph, an autobiographical sketch, a brief interview, the student's favorite book by a professional author, and pages from the various stages of one of the student's pieces.
- Another way to celebrate student writing is to hold a Young Authors' Exhibition or Conference in the school, a public library, or a local community center. This fair could include booths, exhibits, special presentations, and entertainment. Individual students, classrooms, grade levels, or entire schools could submit their best published work in categories such as fiction, essay, research, poetry, drama, biography, and interview. Work would be shared through readings, panels, discussions, and displays. Prizes could be awarded for excellence (rather than "best") in the different categories as well as in illustration, design, and general creativity. All participants could be given a small prize or certificate of participation. This kind of event is fun for all who participate and helps bring the community together.

Publishing Checklist

The following checklist will help students when they are publishing their work. (Not every question applies to every form of publishing.)

- ☑ Have I revised my work to make it better?
- ☑ Have I proofread it carefully?
- ☑ Have I decided upon my illustrations?
- ☑ Have I recopied my piece carefully and illustrated it?
- ☑ Have I numbered the pages?
- ☑ Have I made a cover that tells the title and my name?

Tips

- You will read through the piece, and tell the student if any corrections still need to be made. You may also make some suggestions about the best way to publish a piece if a student has trouble coming up with an idea.
- Make suggestions and give criticism as needed, but remember that students must retain ownership of their publishing. Leave final decisions about form and design of their work up to individual students.
- Remind students to think about their intended audience when they are deciding on the form for their published piece. Will the form they have selected present their ideas effectively to the people they want to reach?

What Does Writing Instruction Look Like in the Classroom?

Instruction and Modeling

The following activities are hallmarks of a quality writing program.

- **Instruction** Teachers teach the fundamentals of the skills of writing (grammar, usage, mechanics, spelling, penmanship); the forms and structures of writing (genre, structures of writing, writer's craft); and the writing process (getting ideas, planning, drafting, revising, editing/proofreading, publishing).
- **Models of Good Writing** Teachers provide models of good writing in each form.
- **Teacher Model** Teachers model all phases of the writing process.
- **Writing Frequency** Students practice writing in different forms frequently, applying the skills in the context of writing.
- **Assessment** Multiple measures of assessment are used, including portfolio and on-demand writing, as well as assessment of writing.

In addition, the following elements promote writing fluency and literacy.

Writing Area

A Writing Area, Writing Folders, and some **simple rules** not only eliminate management problems but also foster independence, encourage risk taking, and cultivate sharing. Work on these as a class at the beginning of the year and feel free to make changes as needed throughout the year.

A Writing Area promotes independence and provides teachers with more time to hold conferences with students. You may find that one Writing Area may become congested, but several different areas may reduce student jams and competition for resources. Students can work alone or in small groups. Have students participate in setting up these areas so they feel involved. It is important that students know what materials are in each center and how to use them.

Materials or Supply Area This area contains a variety of writing materials including pencils, pens, crayons, and unlined paper of different sizes that can be used for drafting as well as for final copies. This is a good opportunity to use recycled paper in your school. Also, computer paper that has alternating green and white lines is great for drafting.

Help Area The materials in this area support independent writing. This is a good place to keep a list of "How to Develop Good Ideas for Writing," as well as books and magazines for authors to browse through for ideas. Checklists for revising and editing, as well as information about genre and literary techniques, enable writers to monitor and check work in progress. After the reading and discussion of a particular genre, let the students know that the information will be at the Help Area in the Writing Area, and encourage them to use it any time during writing. This is also a good place to keep a list of revising and proofreading symbols and dictionaries.

Publishing Area This area contains a variety of materials, including cardboard, folders, tagboard, construction paper, and wallpaper samples for covers; magazines for photos; paints, crayons, and markers for illustrating; stencils for titles; and string, yarn, dental floss, staplers, and punches for binding. Students can bring in pictures of themselves to use for their biographical sketches. Many teachers enlist the help of the school librarian for circulation cards and pockets for students to put on their newly published books. Samples of favorite commercially published books like pop-up books, picture books, and books of different shapes can be included to provide ideas. Materials here are unlimited.

Reading Area Some teachers like to have a separate Reading Area. Often when children are at a loss for writing ideas, browsing through commercially published books or student-published books, as well as magazines and newspapers, can stimulate writers to find new topics to write about.

Writing Folders

Writing Folders help keep writing organized. Every student should have a Writing Folder in which to keep drafts, revisions, and pieces that need a rest. Students also may want to keep a list of ideas for writing, as well as checklists for revising and editing. Folders can be used by teachers for evaluation and for showing parents how their children are growing and exploring different types of writing. Many young authors like to personalize their folders. This can serve as an introductory writing activity.

One concern teachers often express is that folders get messy, and they wonder if a notebook might work better. Notebooks, unfortunately, do not serve the same purpose that folders do. Notebooks discourage students from looking back and comparing drafts. It's nice to have earlier drafts right there next to the page on which the writer is working.

Following are a few simple hints to help students manage their folders.

- Have students put their names and dates on each piece and have them note whether it's a first draft, a revision, or an edited piece. If it is a revision, use a paper clip to hold the draft and revision together.
- Students may want to list the titles of their works somewhere on their Writing Folders.
- Periodically, authors may want to go through their folders and clean them out by removing drafts of published works or pieces that no longer interest the author. Students should be thoughtful and not throw everything away. Small-group conferences in which students talk about why they are keeping some items and throwing others away may be helpful.
- Keep all the students' folders in a central location, like a file drawer or a plastic storage container, to help avoid folders getting mutilated and papers falling out of desks.

Regular feedback encourages young authors to solve problems and make meaningful changes throughout the writing process.

Providing Feedback: Writing Conferences and Seminars

Feedback is one of the most powerful tools for helping writers. Writers want to know how their works in progress sound to someone else, if their stories make sense, if there is any incorrect or misleading information, and where and how to make changes. In ***Open Court,*** opportunities for feedback occur naturally throughout the process as teachers confer with authors during writing and as teachers and peers react to authors' stories during Seminar. Regular feedback encourages young authors to solve problems and make meaningful changes throughout the writing process. This is in marked contrast to feedback that comes only in the final stages when the proud author, after all the hard work has been done, may be overwhelmed and discouraged by teacher and peer feedback. Both **writing conferences** and **seminars** provide students with the opportunity to discuss their work in progress, to share ideas for improvement, and to solve problems.

Conferences offer an excellent opportunity for the teacher and students to evaluate jointly each student's progress and to set goals for future growth.

Writing Conferences

Writing conferences help students identify and solve problems, evaluate their writing, and make changes. Teachers may initiate conferences, but writers should be encouraged to call conferences on an as-needed basis. Because conferences can be held at various times throughout the writing process, the focus will vary. Conferences held during the early stages help students identify and refine a topic or identify research references. During revision, conferences can help students learn to elaborate and reorganize a piece, and during the final stages, to edit and proofread stories before they are published. Conferences offer an excellent opportunity for the teacher and students to evaluate jointly each student's progress and to set goals for future growth.

As teachers circulate throughout the room working with students, they often notice common problems, a discussion of which would benefit the whole class. This is a perfect time to gather students together and have one student present the problem and its possible solution to the others. These are naturally occurring opportunities. Once, when a teacher was conferring with a third grader who was revising a piece, the student decided to add several sentences. Unfortunately, there was not enough room on the paper and the young author, with a look of dismay, said to the teacher, "I have no room. This means copying this page all over again." Sharing a simple trick of the trade, the teacher suggested that the student write the new sentences on a separate piece of paper and mark it "A." Then, the student made a caret, or insertion mark, with an "A" in a circle above it to show where the new sentences would go. This was a revelation. All kinds of things can be added without recopying! The teacher had the student share this new technique with the rest of the class, many of whom eagerly applied it to their own revision activities. The teacher not only captured the moment wisely, but also, by letting the young author do the teaching, encouraged ownership and made the technique relevant.

Peer conferencing should be encouraged during Workshop.

In order to support conferences, you might want to set aside a special area of the classroom for you to work with students or for students to work with each other. During the year, peer conferencing should be encouraged during Workshop. As students engage in peer conferencing, note which students are participating, the types of questions they ask, and the comments they make.

Writing conferences are useful during all phases of the writing process, but they are crucial during the revising phase. Writing conferences give you an opportunity to observe the students as they evaluate their writing, solve problems, make decisions about their work, and take responsibility for the development and completion of their work.

Procedures

The basic procedure for writing conferences is as follows.

1. Have the student read his or her first draft aloud. Offer a specific comment.
2. Encourage the student to review feedback received on his or her draft during peer conferencing or Seminar and to think aloud about possible changes.
3. Identify positive elements of the work.
4. Ask questions that will help the student clarify her or his thinking about how to revise. (Try not to lead the student with content questions. You want to teach how to revise, not what to write.)
5. Review strategies and references that the student could use to improve her or his work.
6. Conclude the conference by having the student state his or her plan or goal for continuing work on the piece.

Writing conferences give you an opportunity to observe the students as they evaluate their writing, solve problems, make decisions about their work, and take responsibility for the development and completion of their work.

During writing conferences, the following responses to student writing might be used.

- **To open communication with the writer:**
  ✓ *How is the writing going?*
  ✓ *Tell me about your piece.*
  ✓ *How did you get your ideas?*
- **To validate the writer's work and give encouragement:**
  ✓ *I like the part where . . .*
  ✓ *I like how you open your piece by . . .*
  ✓ *I like your description of . . .*
- **To get the writer to think about clarity of meaning:**
  ✓ *I wonder about . . .*
  ✓ *What happened after . . .?*
  ✓ *Why did . . .?*
- **To get the writer to think about direction and about writing strategies:**
  ✓ *What do you plan to do with your piece?*
  ✓ *How will you go about doing that?*
  ✓ *What could I do to help you?*

Concentrate on one phase of the writing process at a time. Pay particular attention to revising content, proofreading, or publishing.

Remember to keep conferences brief and to the point. Teachers should prepare their comments in advance if they call the conference. Usually, a student will request the conference. Be sure to confer regularly with every student if only to check that each one is continuing to write, revise, and publish.

Revision Strategy

The following are some strategies to use to encourage students to revise.

- Have students explain how they got their ideas.
- Have students think aloud about how they will address the feedback they have received.

- Ask students to help you understand any confusion you may have about their writing.
- Have the student add, delete, or rearrange something in the work and ask how it affects the whole piece.
- Think aloud while you do a part of what the student was asked to do. Then ask the child to compare what you did to what he or she did.
- Have the student prescribe as if to a younger student how to revise the work.

Writing Conference Questions

Writing conference comments and questions should help students reflect on their work, the process, and how to solve problems.

Following are suggested writing conference comments and questions to help you get started.

Ideas

- Who is your audience?
- What is your purpose for writing?
- How does the reader know what your purpose is?
- Do you have enough information about the topic?
- Do you like one part of your work more than the rest? Why?
- Is your main idea clear?
- Is there a better way to express this idea?
- Is this a good topic sentence?
- Is your introduction engaging?
- Are any important details left out?
- Are any not-so-important details left in?
- Do you use specific vivid details and examples to support your ideas?
- Are your ideas accurate and, if necessary, supported by research?
- Does your conclusion summarize or restate your purpose for writing?
- What might be another way to end the work?
- Tell me about your story. How was the story you told different from what you wrote? (This can lead naturally into revision.)
- I'm having trouble visualizing what you wrote. What other information can you give me?
- You're writing a fairy tale, but you don't know what else to write. What have we learned in reading that will help you? (Going to the Writing Area and looking up characteristics of fairy tales may be a good start.)
- You're writing a newspaper article but don't have enough information. What are some ways of solving that problem? (Try

doing some more reading, talking with the librarian or someone who knows about the content area, or interviewing someone.)

Organization

- Have you organized your writing in a way that makes the most sense based on the main idea you have chosen?
- Is your structure clear so that your reader can follow it? Is there a clear beginning, middle, and conclusion?
- Are there smooth transitions from one part to the next?
- Are supporting details ordered in the most logical way?
- Do you include strong transitions to move the reader smoothly from one paragraph to the next?
- Can you combine any smaller paragraphs or separate larger ones?
- During Seminar, the group felt your story was too long. What kinds of things could you do? (Make two stories or use chapters.)

Voice

- Do you sound confident and knowledgeable?
- Does the voice you use reflect the purpose of your writing? Does your writing sound funny or serious when you want it to be?
- Is your voice appropriate for your audience?
- Do you sound interested in the subject or topic?
- Have you confidently stated your opinion if necessary? Have you used the pronoun "I" if appropriate?
- Does your writing sound like you? Change any overly complex words to simple words whenever possible.
- Is your voice too formal or informal?
- Will this writing get a strong response from the reader?
- Does your writing make the reader care about your topic?

Word Choice

- Do you use the same word or phrase over and over?
- How could you say the same thing in different words?
- Have you defined words your audience may not understand?
- Have you used precise words to describe or explain?
- Is there a better word to express this idea?
- Have you used your own words and phrases when summarizing information from another text?
- Do you use time-order words such as *first, next, then,* and *last* to help the reader understand when events take place?
- Have you used original and memorable words in some places?

Sentence Fluency

- Are your sentences clear and to the point?
- Have you used different kinds and lengths of sentences to effectively present your ideas?
- Would any of your sentences be better if they were shorter?
- Could any of your sentences be combined?
- Is there a rhythm to your sentences?
- Does each sentence introduce a new idea or a new piece of information?
- Do some sentences repeat what has already been stated? If so, cut or change them.
- Have you used transition words such as *in contrast, however,* and *on the other hand* to move smoothly from one subject to another?

- Have you used transitional phrases, such as *according to*, *in addition to*, or *at the same time* to link sentences?
- Have you used conjunctions such as *and*, *but*, and *or* to combine short, choppy sentences?

Tips

- Teachers don't have to meet with every student every day or read every piece each student writes.
- Conferences should be brief; don't overwhelm students with too many comments or suggestions. Several short conferences are often more effective than one long one.
- If appropriate, suggest that students take some notes to help them remember where changes are to be made.
- Don't take ownership of the students' works. Encourage students to identify what is good and what needs to be changed, and let the students make the changes.
- Focus on what is good about the students' works; discuss how to solve problems rather than telling the student what to do.
- Concentrate on the process that students are using, not just the product. Make comments or ask authors questions that encourage them to identify problems and to come up with their own solutions.
- Have sign-up sheets for students who need help each day.
- Identify students with particular strengths in revising and editing, and appoint them as student, or peer, editors.

Seminar

Seminar provides yet another opportunity for students to receive feedback. Seminar is a class discussion of the work of two or three student authors, called Seminar leaders, chosen to share their work each day. As each Seminar leader reads his or her piece, the rest of the class is listening, and a few students will have the chance to comment when the author is finished. In the beginning, teachers may want to choose the Seminar leaders. They may be students who have novel topics, who have written in a particular form, who are revising, who have sloppy first drafts, and so on. After the first few weeks, post a class list, taking three students each day in the order in which their names appear on the list. Initially, it may be necessary to remind students who will be the Seminar leader, but gradually turn the responsibility over to the class. As the year progresses, students may want to hold small-group Seminars during Workshop.

Seminar is an important part of the writing process. Students may use Seminar to brainstorm ideas for writing, to get suggestions for revision, or to focus on a particular problem.

Seminar should accomplish the following:

- Provide opportunities to share and learn from each other.
- Encourage discussion and problem solving.
- Foster a sense of community.
- Allow students to share all their writing at any point in the writing process, not just work they are going to publish.
- Make students responsible for thinking and learning about writing.
- Reinforce all the language arts.
- Develop self-esteem and self-confidence.

Set up some simple rules at the beginning of the year.

1. The Seminar leader selects who will speak from among those who have raised their hands, including the teacher.
2. Seminar participants must listen carefully and provide constructive feedback. Participants should focus on what was good about a piece and ways to make it better.

3. The author has ownership and can decide which suggestions to use. The author does not have to incorporate all suggestions from participants.

Seminar usually occurs before publishing so authors can apply the feedback to their work. Comments and questions from classmates should focus on constructive changes. Be sure to model responses and questions that emphasize the *process*, not just the details in the story. As happens with writing conferences, feedback from Seminar encourages authors to grow.

Seminar for kindergarten writers initially may be sharing pictures and labels. Suggestions during Seminar may relate to comments about changing or adding to the pictures. Gradually, as children start writing words and sentences, the focus will shift to comments about the text. In the upper grades, as students start writing and sharing longer pieces of writing, they may want to share only part of a piece. When they do this, the authors should explain why they have chosen a particular section; for example, it's a part they particularly like or one with which they are having problems. Remember, students should use Seminar to share their research in progress, as well. During Seminar, students can get feedback on their research, refine their questions, and discuss problems such as finding resources.

Following are some examples of comments to try.

- I'd like to hear more about . . . (Stimulates writers to say more.)
- I wasn't sure what you meant about . . . (Encourages authors to clarify thoughts and ideas.)

- I like the part in your drawing where . . . My favorite part was . . . (Provides a good starting point for the Seminar.)
- What would you see if you had taken a picture of that? (Helps authors add information.)
- How else can you let us know that the dog was happy? (Encourages authors to say the same thing in different ways.)
- How are all the ideas in this section alike? What can you do with the ones that don't fit? (Helps authors organize ideas and develop paragraphs.)
- How did you come up with this topic? Why did you decide to write on it? (Helps students focus on process and think about different ideas for writing.)
- What have you learned from reading or from other student authors that will help you solve this problem? (Focuses on the reading/writing connection, problem solving, and process.)

Initially, the teacher is the primary responder to the Seminar leaders, but after a couple of weeks, students begin to take over.

If student comments begin to get stale or if they ask the same questions routinely, the teacher should interject new ways of thinking about writing by modeling additional comments and questions.

Initially, the teacher is the primary responder to the Seminar leaders, but after a couple of weeks, students begin to take over.

Ownership of work is important. Each student author decides whether or not to incorporate some or all of the Seminar suggestions into his or her writing and research. One reason students may appear reluctant to incorporate changes is because they are hit with a number of possible suggestions, some of which they forget by the time they get back to their writing. A couple of recommendations may help here. First of all, the teacher may want to take some notes to share during a subsequent conference. Or, a peer can act as a secretary who takes notes and then helps the author decide if, where, and how to make changes. Another idea is to allow the Seminar leader to leave the group and start making changes immediately while the ideas are still fresh.

Following are some practical tips from teachers.

- Have a chair designated as the "Author's Chair" from which the Seminar leaders can read their work. This lends importance to the activity.
- Each Seminar leader should be encouraged to give a bit of background, including where he or she is in the process, why he or she chose a particular part, or what problem he or she is having. This helps orient the class listeners.
- Short stories can be read in their entirety. As students become more proficient and write longer stories, they should be encouraged to read just a part of the work; for example, one they need help with, one that has been revised, or one they particularly like.
- Take notes during Seminar and encourage older students to do the same. Teachers also may keep an ongoing record of Seminar participants, dates, story topics, and stages of development.
- Be sensitive to the attention span of the class and the feedback being given. There is a tendency sometimes for students to repeat the same comments to each author. Encourage students to listen carefully, not just to the Seminar leader but to each other as well. Teachers may want to limit the number of student responders the leader calls on to four or five.
- Once students understand the concept of Seminar and are thinking critically about each other's writing, small-group seminars can be held in which everyone in the group has the chance to share. These can be initiated by either the teacher or the students.
- Before Seminar is held, have leaders briefly record information on a record sheet, including the topic or title, the kind of story, where she or he is in the process (drafting, revising, editing), problems, and so on. This encourages students to think about their Seminar presentations before they get up to read. It fosters responsibility and becomes a record sheet for the teacher as well.

The goal of writing in ***Open Court*** is to develop independent, self-directed writers. Comments and questions during writing conferences and Seminar should be constructive and should encourage students to reflect on their work and take responsibility for making changes.

Comments and questions during writing conferences and Seminar should be constructive and should encourage students to reflect on their work and take responsibility for making changes.

Evaluating the Process: Learning from Writing

Opportunities for evaluating writing are built into ***Open Court.*** Writing Folders contain an ongoing record of each student's work. Writing conferences give teachers time to observe students as they evaluate their writing, solve problems, make decisions about their work, and take responsibility for the development and completion of pieces. The focus is on the process, not just the correctness of the written story.

Evaluation Through Conferences

Writing conferences provide a nonthreatening time to observe authors as they think aloud about problems and solutions and demonstrate their understanding of the writing process. During discussions, listen for the following cues that indicate growth.

- The author identifies problems.
- The author talks about strategies and solutions and why they may or may not work.

- The author is making thoughtful changes.
- The author can identify unnecessary details.
- The author recognizes how and when the text needs to be reorganized.
- The author identifies places that need elaboration. Young authors initially do this by adding on at the end and later by inserting information.
- The author spontaneously changes or revises after reading a piece to you.
- The author makes use of books, the Writing Area, peers, and other resources.
- The emergent author notes the need for labeling, adding to his or her picture, or dictating a story.

Some teachers like to hold formal evaluation conferences with students. Be sure to involve the students in the process by having them select the piece or pieces to be evaluated. Try asking *some* of the following questions that focus on understanding and lead to change.

- Why did you choose this piece?
- What makes it good or interesting?
- What problems did you have writing this piece?
- How did you solve those problems?
- How did you revise this piece after you wrote the initial draft?

- How did you follow through on the writing process?
- What new things did you learn from writing this piece or during this marking period?
- What are your plans for the next marking period?
- What new ideas do you plan to explore?

After the writing conference, it is helpful for the teacher and the student to put the results of the conference in writing and keep a copy of it in the student's Writing Folder. This can be used for the next evaluation conference and also is good to share with parents.

Periodically, teachers may formally evaluate the students' writing. The Analytical Scoring Rubric on page 44 is a scale that can be used to help evaluate student writing and monitor growth during the year.

Evaluation Through Seminar

Seminar is a good time to observe both the Seminar leader and class participants. Notice which students are participating, the kinds of questions they ask, and the comments they make. These are often good indicators of students' understanding of writing. Take a few minutes after Seminar to confer with Seminar leaders to find out if they are evaluating class suggestions and are responding to audience concerns by incorporating some of the suggestions in their work.

Evaluation Using Writing Folders

Students' Writing Folders present an excellent opportunity for evaluation because they contain samples of students' writing over a period of time. In reviewing students' work, look for changes that indicate growth in understanding of the process, rather than looking only for correctness. When comparing pieces, here are some ideas to keep in mind.

In reviewing students' work, look for changes that indicate growth in understanding of the process, rather than looking only for correctness.

- Does the work in the folders show versatility? What different types of writing has the author tried or completed?
- How does the work reflect drafting, revising, editing, and publishing?
- What different approaches to revision and editing are found?
- In the early grades, how is the young author showing growth from scribbles to pictures, and to pictures with labels that use invented spelling?
- How does the student's writing reflect more sophisticated thinking?
- How do pieces reflect the author's use of strategies; for example, do works contain different types of elaboration like dialogue, description, and extended sentences?

- How does the writing reflect the development of ideas and the growth of knowledge?
- Does the revising reflect growth in problem solving?
- How is the author integrating ideas from reading into writing?

When reviewing student folders, teachers don't necessarily have to read everything every student writes. Many teachers work with their students to develop writing portfolios that contain samples of each student's work. Criteria can be set up that will help the student, or the teacher and student together, make selections for the portfolio. Pieces may be the students' best work, most interesting piece, most challenging piece, most unusual piece, piece that showed the most improvement, and so on. Also include copies of drafts, revisions, and the like. Letting the students make the final selection encourages them to reflect on their work yet another time and involves them in the evaluation process right from the start.

Many teachers send these portfolios with the students' records to the teachers the students will have the next year. What better way to find out about your new students' understanding of writing than through their own words!

Writing Assessments

Rubrics

A rubric is an established rule or criterion. It sets goals for students that are clearly stated, attainable, observable, and measurable. A rubric clearly describes the attributes across a range of age-appropriate performance. Rubrics established before an assignment is given are extremely helpful in evaluating the assignment. They take away much of the arbitrary and subjective nature of assessment that makes both students and teachers uneasy.

When students know what the rubrics for a particular assignment are, they can focus their energies on the key issues. In addition, rubrics give the teacher and the student an ultimate goal, so that at all times both can be working toward the most sophisticated level on the scale. It is continual movement toward this goal that assures overall success for the students.

Writing rubrics can provide guidance for students and teachers with a structure for creating and evaluating written work. Following are the rubrics for writing used in ***Open Court Reading***.

Writing Rubrics Grades 1–2

	1 Point	2 Points	3 Points	4 Points
Conventions				
Conventions (Overall grammar, usage, mechanics, and spelling)	Demonstrates no evidence of English language conventions.	Demonstrates limited but inconsistent use of English language conventions.	Demonstrates emerging consistent use of English language conventions such as capitalization and end punctuation.	Demonstrates consistent use and awareness of English language conventions.
Grammar and Usage	Demonstrates minimal awareness of standard usage.	Demonstrates some awareness of standard usage.	Demonstrates emerging awareness of standard usage and subject/verb agreement.	Includes standard usage and demonstrates understanding of subject/verb agreement in writing.
Mechanics: Punctuation	Makes little use of punctuation.	Uses periods correctly for end punctuation.	Uses most end punctuation correctly.	Uses end punctuation and some commas correctly.
Mechanics: Capitalization	Inconsistently uses capital letters.	Inconsistently uses capitals at beginning of sentences and for some proper nouns.	Capitalizes sentences; may overcapitalize or undercapitalize other words.	Uses capitalization correctly at beginning of sentences and with proper nouns.
Sentence Structure	Writes words or labels but not sentences.	Writes very simple sentences.	Uses sentences to express ideas in writing.	Uses simple and complex or compound sentences to express ideas.
Spelling	Mainly uses invented spellings.	Uses sound spelling as a primary strategy. Many words are misspelled.	Uses many correct sound spellings and uses some structural spelling patterns.	Uses mostly correct sound spellings and structural patterns.
Genre				
Descriptive Writing	Includes little or no description of setting, character, or motivations.	Includes minimal description.	Includes adequate detail description.	Includes sensory details, motivations, and scenery details that add depth of understanding.
Expository Structure	Writing consists of ideas loosely related to a topic, with no evident order or organization. Extraneous material may be present.	Statements have an evident purpose (to describe, explain, argue, etc.).	Main points and supportive details can be identified but they are not clearly marked.	Composition is clearly organized around main points with supportive facts or assertions.
Genre	Writing does not reflect any particular genre. A story is indistinguishable from a persuasive or expository composition.	Writing has minimal elements of genre.	Writing adequately reflects structure of a particular genre.	Writing develops around elements and structure of a specific genre.
Narrative	Narrative has missing details or elements (characterization, plot, setting). Logical order is not apparent.	Includes plot outline but does not elaborate on details of character, plot, or setting.	Adequately develops plot, character, and setting.	Fully develops and elaborates on plot, character, and setting.
Narrative Character	Minimal awareness of character beyond self is included.	Characters are named but not defined or described.	Identifies, describes, and compares story characters in terms of basic categorical descriptors such as *nice* or *mean.*	Describes characters in increasing detail in original stories, including both physical and mental qualities such as *strength* or *kindness.*
Narrative Plot	Story is a sequence of events that may or may not be related.	Story is a sequence of events in chronological order.	Plot includes problem and its resolution, which moves logically through time.	Plot is developed with a problem, failed attempts, complications, and subproblems before resolution. Plot moves logically through time.

Writing Rubrics Grades 1–2 (continued)

	1 Point	2 Points	3 Points	4 points
Narrative Setting	Story includes no description of setting.	Minimal elements of setting are included.	Creates settings that include descriptions of time, character, and place.	Adds details that make setting distinctive and appropriate to the story type (fantasy vs. realistic settings).
Persuasive	Position is absent or confusing. Insufficient writing to show that criteria are met.	Position is vague or lacks clarity. Unrelated ideas or multiple positions are included.	An opening statement identifies position. Writing may develop fewer or more points than delineated in opening. Focus may be too broad.	Sets scope and purpose of position in introduction. Maintains position throughout. Supports arguments. Includes effective closing.
Personal	Minimal effort is made and writing does not reflect writer's ideas.	Some elements of personal writing reflect writer's thoughts and ideas.	Writer uses personal writing to record or develop thoughts.	Writer relies on personal writing to record, remember, develop, or express writer's thoughts.
Poetry	Little effort is made to select and arrange words to express a particular thought or idea. The main idea of the poem is not evident.	Some effort is made to work with word choice and arrangement to develop a thought in poetry form.	Writer has a clear idea to express in a poem and has attempted to use poetic form to express it. Poetry form may reflect established forms.	Writer has expressed an idea in an original or established poetic form. Writer has carefully selected words and arranged them for poetic effect.
The Writing Process				
Getting Ideas	Shows little awareness that own ideas are the material of writing.	Consciously calls on own experience and knowledge for ideas in writing.	Is aware that writing requires thinking about content and ideas.	Evaluates and alters ideas as writing proceeds.
Prewriting—Organizing Writing	Makes little or no attempt to develop a plan for writing.	Uses a given model to plan writing.	Elaborates on the model for planning.	Develops own plan based on the model.
Drafting	Writes without attention to plan or is unable to write.	Writes a minimal amount with some attention to plan.	Uses plan to draft.	Elaborates on plan in drafting.
Revising	Quickly finishes writing products and doesn't seek feedback.	Pays attention as teacher provides feedback about written work.	Welcomes feedback and advice from teacher or other students.	Actively seeks feedback from other students and teacher.
Editing	Demonstrates no attention to correcting grammar, usage, mechanics, or spelling errors.	Some errors in English language conventions are corrected. Many are not corrected.	Corrects many errors in English language conventions.	Corrects most errors in English language conventions. Uses resources or seeks assistance to address uncertainties.
Presentation/ Publishing	Presents revised and edited draft as final.	Recopies final draft with no extra presentation.	Includes adequate presentation efforts with illustration, format, and style.	Provides impressive presentation of written work with attention to format, style, illustration, and clarity.
Self-Management	Puts writing tasks off until the last minute and seldom finishes work on time.	Allows some, but often not enough, time for writing tasks.	Allows time for writing but not enough for planning, gathering information, etc.	Listens to advice about time requirements and plans accordingly.
Language Resources	Seldom refers to language resources such as word walls or dictionaries.	Asks teacher or other students for help with words.	When reminded, uses classroom resources such as word walls and dictionaries.	Makes active use of varied classroom language resources.

	I Point	2 Points	3 Points	4 points
Writing Traits				
Audience	Displays little or no sense of audience.	Displays some sense of audience.	Writes with audience in mind throughout.	Displays a strong sense of audience. Engages audience.
Citing Sources	Does not understand the difference between one's own work and the work of others. Clearly copies the work of others.	Uses others' work as a model.	Writes one's own words and refrains from copying the work of others.	Takes pride in one's own words and acknowledges ideas of others.
Elaboration (supporting details and examples that develop the main idea)	Little or no elaboration of detail.	Minimal detail.	Includes sufficient detail to develop or support ideas.	Elaborates on ideas with supporting details.
Focus	No focus is present. Main idea cannot be inferred.	Topic/position/direction is unclear or reader has to infer.	Topic/position is stated and direction/purpose is previewed and maintained. Mainly stays on topic.	Topic/position is clearly stated, previewed, and maintained throughout the paper. Topics and details are tied together.
Ideas/Content	Superficial and/or minimal content is included.	The reader can understand the main ideas although they may be overly broad or simplistic, and the results may not be effective. Supporting detail is limited, insubstantial, overly general, or off topic.	The writing is clear and focused. The reader can easily understand the main ideas. Support is present, although it may be limited or rather general.	Writing is exceptionally clear, focused, and interesting. Main ideas stand out and are developed by strong support and rich details.
Organization	Organization is not apparent.	An attempt has been made to organize the writing. Writing may be a listing of facts/ideas.	Organization is clear and coherent. Beginning or conclusion is included.	The organization develops the central idea. The order and structure move the reader through the text easily. Beginning grabs attention. Conclusion adds impact. Uses a variety of transitions that enhance meaning.
Sentence Fluency	The writing is difficult to follow.	The writing tends to be mechanical rather than fluid.	The writing flows, however connections between phrases or sentences may be less than fluid.	The writing has an effective flow and rhythm. Sentence patterns are somewhat varied, contributing to ease in oral reading.
Voice	The writing provides little sense of involvement or commitment. There is no evidence that the writer has chosen a suitable voice.	The writer's commitment to the topic seems inconsistent. A sense of the writer may emerge at times; however, the voice is either inappropriately personal or inappropriately impersonal.	A voice is present. The writer demonstrates commitment to the topic. In places, the writing is expressive, engaging, or sincere. Words and expressions are clear and precise.	The writer has chosen a voice appropriate for the topic, purpose, and audience. Unique style comes through. The writing is expressive, engaging, or sincere. Exhibits strong commitment to the topic.
Word Choice	The writing shows an extremely limited vocabulary and frequent misuse of words.	Language is ordinary, filled with familiar words and phrases. Exhibits minimal word usage. Words and expressions are clear, but usually more general than specific.	Words effectively convey the intended message. Exhibits adequate word usage. Contains some interesting words. Includes some vivid, descriptive language.	Words convey the intended message in an interesting, precise, and natural way appropriate to audience and purpose. Exhibits exceptional word usage. Frequently includes interesting words.

Writing Rubrics Grades 3–4

	1 Point	2 Points	3 Points	4 Points
Conventions				
Conventions (Overall grammar, usage, mechanics, and spelling)	Numerous errors in usage, grammar, spelling, capitalization, and punctuation repeatedly distract the reader and make the text difficult to read. The reader finds it difficult to focus on the message.	The writing demonstrates limited control of standard writing conventions (punctuation, spelling, capitalization, paragraph breaks, grammar, and usage). Errors sometimes impede readability.	The writing demonstrates control of standard writing conventions (punctuation, spelling, capitalization, paragraph breaks, grammar, and usage). Minor errors, while perhaps noticeable, do not impede readability.	The writing demonstrates exceptionally strong control of standard writing conventions (punctuation, spelling, capitalization, paragraph breaks, grammar, and usage) and uses them effectively to enhance communication. Errors are so few and so minor that the reader can easily skim over them.
Grammar and Usage	Writing shows lack of awareness of standard usage and has many errors in subject-verb agreement.	Writing demonstrates some awareness of standard usage and proper sentence structure.	Writing mainly includes standard usage and correct sentence structure.	Writing uses a variety of sentence structures appropriately for effect and demonstrates understanding of standard usage.
Mechanics: Punctuation	Uses periods correctly, but makes little use of other punctuation.	Uses end punctuation correctly.	Uses most punctuation correctly.	Uses end punctuation, commas, quotation marks, parentheses, ellipses, and other forms of punctuation correctly and appropriately.
Mechanics: Capitalization	Inconsistently uses capitals at beginnings of sentences and seldom uses them for proper nouns.	Consistently uses capitals at beginnings of sentences and for some proper nouns.	Capitalizes sentences; may overcapitalize or undercapitalize other words.	Uses capitalization correctly at beginnings of sentences, with proper nouns, and in titles.
Sentence Structure	Some sentences are standard, but many are run-on sentences or fragments.	Primarily uses simple sentences. Writing has some run-on sentences or sentence fragments. May use repetitive sentence patterns.	Uses standard sentence construction throughout and a variety of simple and complex sentence patterns. Writing may have a few run-on sentences or sentence fragments.	Uses standard sentence construction throughout. Sentence patterns and length are varied, effective, and enhance what is said. Writing has no unintentional run-on sentences or sentence fragments.
Spelling	Uses sound spelling as a primary strategy. Many words are misspelled.	Uses many correct sound spellings and some structural spelling patterns.	Uses mostly correct sound spellings and structural patterns.	Uses correct sound spelling patterns and structural patterns, and understands affixes and homophones.
Genre				
Descriptive Writing	Includes little or no description of setting, character, or motivations.	Includes minimal description.	Includes adequate detail description.	Includes sensory details, motivations, and scenery details that add depth of understanding.
Expository Structure	Composition consists of statements loosely related to a topic, with no evident order or organization. Extraneous material may be present.	Statements have an evident purpose (to describe, explain, argue, etc.).	Main points and supportive details can be identified but they are not clearly marked.	Composition is clearly organized around main points with supportive facts or assertions.
Genre	Writing does not reflect any particular genre. A story is indistinguishable from a persuasive or expository composition.	Writing has minimal elements of genre.	Writing adequately reflects structure of a particular genre.	Writing develops around elements and structure of a specific genre.

	1 Point	2 Points	3 Points	4 Points
Narrative	Narrative has missing details or elements (characterization, plot, setting). Logical order is not apparent.	Narrative includes plot outline but does not elaborate on details of character, plot, or setting.	Narrative adequately develops plot, character, and setting.	Narrative fully develops and elaborates on plot, character, and setting.
Narrative Character	Identifies, describes, and compares story characters in terms of basic categorical descriptors such as *nice* or *mean.*	Describes characters in increasing detail in original stories, including both physical and mental qualities such as *strength* or *kindness.*	Describes the internal mental world of story characters by explicitly describing thoughts, feelings, and desires.	Creates lifelike characters whose action and speech reflect unique qualities that are integral to the plot.
Narrative Plot	Story is a sequence of events that hang together in chronological order.	Story has a simple plot, comprising problem and resolution. May end abruptly or lack closing. Subject is clear but theme is not. May have major digression or inappropriate transitions that disrupt progression of ideas.	Plot includes problem, failed attempts, subproblems, and resolution. Evidence of coherence and cohesion but may depend on formulaic structure. Subject and theme are clear and maintained.	Plot is elaborated with descriptive details and elements that add excitement or color. Narrative structure is clear—sequence of events moves logically through time with a beginning, middle, and ending, with an effective closing. Subject and theme are clear and developed throughout.
Narrative Setting	Creates simple settings consisting of time *(once upon a time* or *one day)* and/or place for original stories.	Creates settings that include descriptions of time, character, and place.	Adds details that make setting distinctive and are appropriate to the story type (fantasy vs. realistic settings).	Describes settings in ways that contribute to mood, suspense, humor, or excitement of the story.
Narrative Theme	No theme is apparent.	Superficial theme is included but not integrated.	A theme is expressed but not well developed.	The narrative fully develops a theme that expresses an underlying message beyond the narrative plot.
Persuasive	Position is absent or confusing. Insufficient writing to show that criteria are met.	Position is vague or lacks clarity. Unrelated ideas or multiple positions are included.	An opening statement identifies position. Writing may develop fewer or more points than delineated in opening. Focus may be too broad.	Sets scope and purpose of paper in introduction. Maintains position throughout. Supports arguments. Includes effective closing.
Personal	Personal writing is seen as an assignment rather than as an aid to writer. Minimal effort is made and writing does not reflect writer's ideas.	Some elements of personal writing reflect writer's thoughts and ideas.	Writer uses personal writing to record or develop thoughts.	Writer relies on personal writing to record, remember, develop, or express writer's thoughts.
Poetry	Little effort is made to select and arrange words to express a particular thought or idea. The main idea of the poem is not evident.	Some effort is made to work with word choice and arrangement to develop a thought in poetry form.	Writer has a clear idea to express in a poem and has attempted to use poetic form to express it. Poetry form may reflect established forms.	Writer has expressed an idea in an original or established poetic form. Writer has carefully selected words and arranged them for poetic effect.
The Writing Process				
Getting Ideas	Shows little awareness that own ideas are the material of writing.	Consciously calls on own experience and knowledge for ideas in writing.	Is aware that writing requires thinking about content and ideas.	Evaluates and alters ideas as writing proceeds.
Prewriting—Organizing Writing	Makes little or no attempt to develop a plan for writing.	Uses model to plan.	Elaborates on the model for planning.	Develops own plan based on the model.

Writing Rubrics Grades 3–4 (continued)

	1 Point	2 Points	3 Points	4 points
Drafting	Writes without attention to plan or is unable to write.	Writes a minimal amount with some attention to plan.	Uses plan to draft.	Elaborates on plan in drafting.
Revising	Quickly finishes writing products and doesn't seek feedback.	Pays attention as teacher provides feedback about written work.	Welcomes feedback and advice from teacher or other students.	Actively seeks feedback from other students and teacher.
Editing	Demonstrates no attention to correcting grammar, usage, mechanics, or spelling errors.	Some errors in English language conventions are corrected. Many are not corrected.	Corrects many errors in English language conventions.	Corrects most errors in English language conventions. Uses resources or seeks assistance to address uncertainties.
Presentation/ Publishing	Presents revised and edited draft as final.	Recopies final draft with no extra presentation.	Includes adequate presentation efforts with illustration, format, and style.	Impressive presentation of written work with attention to format, style, illustration, and clarity.
Self-Management	Puts writing tasks off until the last minute and seldom finishes work on time.	Allows some, but often not enough, time for writing tasks.	Allows time for writing but not enough for planning, gathering information, etc.	Listens to advice about time requirements and plans accordingly.
Language Resources	Seldom refers to language resources such as word walls or dictionaries.	Asks teacher or other students for help with words.	When reminded, uses classroom resources such as word walls and dictionaries.	Makes active use of varied classroom language resources.
Writing Traits				
Audience	Displays little or no sense of audience. Does not engage audience.	Displays some sense of audience.	Writes with audience in mind throughout.	Displays a strong sense of audience. Engages audience.
Citing Sources	Demonstrates little commitment to the quality and significance of research and the accuracy of the written document. There is no documentation of sources.	Demonstrates limited commitment to the quality and significance of research and the accuracy of the written document. Documentation is sometimes used to avoid plagiarism and to enable the reader to judge how believable or important a piece of information is by checking the source.	Demonstrates commitment to the quality and significance of research and the accuracy of the written document. Documentation is used to avoid plagiarism and to enable the reader to judge how believable or important a piece of information is by checking the source.	Demonstrates exceptionally strong commitment to the quality and significance of research and the accuracy of the written document. Documentation is used to avoid plagiarism and to enable the reader to judge how believable or important a piece of information is by checking the source.
Elaboration (supporting details and examples that develop the main idea)	States ideas or points with minimal detail to support them.	Includes sketchy, redundant, or general details; some may be irrelevant. Support for key ideas is very uneven.	Includes mix of general statements and specific details/examples. Support is mostly relevant but may be uneven and lack depth in places.	Includes specific details and supporting examples for each key point/idea. May use compare/contrast to support.
Focus	Topic is unclear or wanders and must be inferred. Extraneous material may be present.	Topic/position/direction is unclear and must be inferred.	Topic/position is stated and direction/purpose is previewed and maintained. Mainly stays on topic.	Topic/position is clearly stated, previewed, and maintained throughout the paper. Topics and details are tied together with a central theme or purpose that is maintained/threaded throughout the paper.
Ideas/Content	Superficial and/or minimal content is included.	Main ideas are understandable, although they may be overly broad or simplistic, and the results may not be effective. Supporting detail is limited, insubstantial, overly general, or off topic.	The writing is clear and focused. The reader can easily understand the main ideas. Support is present, although it may be limited or rather general.	Writing is exceptionally clear, focused, and interesting. Main ideas stand out and are developed by strong support and rich details.

	1 Point	2 Points	3 Points	4 points
Organization	The writing lacks coherence; organization seems haphazard and disjointed. Plan is not evident. Facts are presented randomly. No transitions are included. Beginning is weak and ending is abrupt. There is no awareness of paragraph structure or organization.	An attempt has been made to organize the writing; however the overall structure is inconsistent or skeletal. Plan is evident but loosely structured or writer overuses a particular pattern. Writing may be a listing of facts/ideas with a weak beginning or conclusion. Transitions are awkward or nonexistent. Includes beginning use of paragraphs.	Organization is clear and coherent. Order and structure are present, but may seem formulaic. Plan is evident. Reasons for the order of key concepts may be unclear. Beginning or conclusion is included but may lack impact. Transitions are present. Paragraph use is appropriate.	The organization enhances the central idea and its development. The order and structure are compelling and move the reader through the text easily. Plan is evident. Key concepts are logically sequenced. Beginning grabs attention. Conclusion adds impact. Uses a variety of transitions that enhance meaning. Uses paragraphs appropriately.
Sentence Fluency	The writing is difficult to follow, either choppy or rambling. Sentences are incomplete or awkward constructions force the reader to slow down or reread.	The writing tends to be mechanical rather than fluid. Occasional awkward constructions may force the reader to slow down.	The writing flows, however connections between phrases or sentences may be less than fluid. Sentence patterns are somewhat varied, contributing to ease in oral reading.	The writing has an effective flow and rhythm. Sentences show a high degree of craftsmanship, with consistently strong and varied structure that makes expressive oral reading easy and enjoyable.
Voice	The writing provides little sense of involvement or commitment. There is no evidence that the writer has chosen a suitable voice. Does not engage audience.	The writer's commitment to the topic seems inconsistent. A sense of the writer may emerge at times; however, the voice is either inappropriately personal or inappropriately impersonal.	A voice is present. The writer demonstrates commitment to the topic. In places, the writing is expressive, engaging, or sincere. Words and expressions are clear and precise.	The writer has chosen a voice appropriate for the topic, purpose, and audience. Unique style comes through. The writing is expressive, engaging, or sincere. Exhibits strong commitment to the topic.
Word Choice	Exhibits less than minimal word usage. The writing shows an extremely limited vocabulary and frequent misuse of words. Language is monotonous. Includes no interesting words. Words and expressions are simple and may be repetitive, inappropriate, or overused.	Exhibits minimal word usage. Language is ordinary, lacking interest, precision, and variety. May be inappropriate to audience and purpose in places. The writing is filled with familiar words and phrases. Contains only a few interesting words. Words and expressions are clear but usually more general than specific.	Exhibits adequate word usage. Words effectively convey the intended message. The writer employs a variety of words that are functional and appropriate to audience and purpose. Contains some interesting words. Includes some vivid, descriptive language.	Exhibits exceptional word usage. Words convey the intended message in an exceptionally interesting, precise, and natural way appropriate to audience and purpose. The writer employs a rich, broad range of words, which have been carefully chosen and thoughtfully placed for impact. Frequently contains interesting words. Uses literary devices effectively.

Writing Rubrics Grades 5–6

	1 Point	2 Points	3 Points	4 Points
Conventions				
Conventions (Overall grammar, usage, mechanics, and spelling)	Numerous errors in usage, grammar, spelling, capitalization, and punctuation repeatedly distract the reader and make the text difficult to read. The reader finds it difficult to focus on the message.	The writing demonstrates limited control of standard writing conventions (punctuation, spelling, capitalization, paragraph breaks, grammar, and usage). Errors sometimes impede readability.	The writing demonstrates control of standard writing conventions (punctuation, spelling, capitalization, paragraph breaks, grammar, and usage). Minor errors, while perhaps noticeable, do not impede readability.	The writing demonstrates exceptionally strong control of standard writing conventions (punctuation, spelling, capitalization, paragraph breaks, grammar, and usage) and uses them effectively to enhance communication. Errors are so few and so minor that the reader can easily skim over them.
Grammar and Usage	Writing shows lack of awareness of standard usage and has many errors in subject-verb agreement.	Writing demonstrates some awareness of standard usage and proper sentence structure.	Writing mainly includes standard usage and correct sentence structure.	Writing uses a variety of sentence structures appropriately for effect and demonstrates understanding of standard usage.
Mechanics: Punctuation	Uses periods correctly but makes little use of other punctuation.	Uses end punctuation correctly.	Uses most punctuation correctly.	Uses end punctuation, commas, quotation marks, parentheses, ellipses, and other forms of punctuation correctly and appropriately.
Mechanics: Capitalization	Uses capitals correctly at beginnings of sentences but inconsistently in other places.	Consistently uses capitals at beginnings of sentences and for some proper nouns.	Mainly uses capitalization correctly.	Uses capitalization correctly in sentences, proper nouns, and titles and demonstrates awareness of capitalization rules in unique situations.
Sentence Structure	Some sentences are standard, but many are run-on sentences or fragments.	Primarily uses simple sentences. Writing has some run-on sentences or sentence fragments. May use repetitive sentence patterns.	Uses standard sentence construction throughout with a variety of simple and complex sentence patterns. Writing may have a few run-on sentences or sentence fragments.	Uses standard sentence construction throughout. Sentence patterns and length are varied, effective, and enhance what is said. Writing has no unintentional run-on sentences or sentence fragments.
Spelling	Uses sound spelling as a primary strategy. Many words are misspelled.	Uses many correct sound spellings and some structural spelling patterns.	Uses mostly correct sound spellings and structural patterns.	Uses correct sound spelling patterns and structural patterns; understands affixes, homophones, and meaning patterns.
Genre				
Descriptive Writing	Includes little or no description of setting, character, or motivations.	Includes minimal description.	Includes adequate detail description.	Includes sensory details, motivations, and scenery details that add depth of understanding.
Expository Structure	Main points and supportive details can be identified, but they are not clearly marked.	Composition is clearly organized around main points with supportive facts or assertions.	Presents adequate, appropriate evidence to make a point or support a position. Positions are compared and contrasted in the course of developing the main point.	Traces and constructs a line of argument, identifying part-to-whole relations. Main points are supported with logical and appropriate evidence.
Genre	Writing does not reflect any particular genre. A story is indistinguishable from a persuasive or expository composition.	Writing has minimal elements of genre.	Writing adequately reflects structure of a particular genre.	Writing develops around elements and structure of a specific genre.

	1 Point	2 Points	3 Points	4 Points
Narrative	Narrative has missing details or elements (characterization, plot, setting). Logical order is not apparent.	Narrative includes plot outline but does not elaborate on details of character, plot, or setting.	Narrative adequately develops plot, character, and setting.	Narrative fully develops and elaborates on plot, character, and setting.
Narrative Character	Describes characters in increasing detail in original stories, including both physical and mental qualities such as *strength* or *kindness*.	Describes the internal mental world of story characters by explicitly describing thoughts, feelings, and desires.	Creates lifelike characters whose action and speech reflect unique qualities that are integral to the plot.	Creates complex characters, identifying psychological traits that are represented throughout the narrative.
Narrative Plot	Plot includes problem, failed attempts, subproblems, and resolution. Evidence of coherence and cohesion but may depend on formulaic structure. Subject and theme are clear and maintained.	Plot is elaborated with descriptive details and elements that add excitement or color. Narrative structure is clear—sequence of events moves logically through time with a beginning, middle, and ending with effective closing. Subject and theme are clear and developed throughout.	Plot is well developed with subplots and complications integrated into the resolution.	Includes more complicated plotlines with varied time lines, flashbacks, or dual story lines.
Narrative Setting	Creates settings that simply include descriptions of time, character, and place.	Describes settings in ways that contribute to the mood, suspense, humor, or excitement of the story.	Identifies how settings influence story problems and their resolutions or contribute to other story elements, such as character and plot.	Creates settings that include metaphoric or symbolic elements that help develop story elements.
Narrative Theme	No theme is apparent.	Superficial theme is included but not integrated.	A theme is expressed but not well developed.	The narrative fully develops a theme that expresses an underlying message beyond the narrative plot.
Persuasive	Position is absent or confusing. Insufficient writing to show that criteria are met.	Position is vague or lacks clarity. Unrelated ideas or multiple positions are included.	An opening statement identifies position. Writing may develop fewer or more points than delineated in opening. Focus may be too broad.	Sets scope and purpose of paper in introduction. Maintains position throughout. Supports arguments. Includes effective closing.
Personal	Personal writing is seen as an assignment rather than as an aid to writer. Minimal effort is made and writing does not reflect writer's ideas.	Some elements of personal writing reflect writer's thoughts and ideas.	Writer uses personal writing to record or develop thoughts.	Writer relies on personal writing to record, remember, develop, or express writer's thoughts.
Poetry	Little effort is made to select and arrange words to express a particular thought or idea. The main idea of the poem is not evident.	Some effort is made to work with word choice and arrangement to develop a thought in poetry form.	Writer has a clear idea to express in a poem and has attempted to use poetic form to express it. Poetry form may reflect established forms.	Writer has expressed an idea in an original or established poetic form. Writer has carefully selected words and arranged them for poetic effect.
The Writing Process				
Getting Ideas	Shows little awareness that own ideas are the material of writing.	Consciously calls on own experience and knowledge for ideas in writing.	Is aware that writing requires thinking about content and ideas.	Evaluates and alters ideas as writing proceeds.
Prewriting—Organizing Writing	Makes little or no attempt to develop a plan for writing.	Uses model to plan.	Elaborates on the model for planning.	Develops own plan based on the model.

Writing Rubrics Grades 5–6 (continued)

	1 Point	2 Points	3 Points	4 Points
Drafting	Writes without attention to plan or is unable to write.	Writes a minimal amount with some attention to plan.	Uses plan to draft.	Elaborates on plan in drafting.
Revising	Quickly finishes writing products and doesn't seek feedback.	Pays attention as teacher provides feedback about written work.	Welcomes feedback and advice from teacher or other students.	Actively seeks feedback from other students and teacher.
Editing	Demonstrates no attention to correcting grammar, usage, mechanics, or spelling errors.	Some errors in English language conventions are corrected. Many are not corrected.	Corrects many errors in English language conventions.	Corrects most errors in English language conventions. Uses resources or seeks assistance to address uncertainties.
Presentation/ Publishing	Presents revised and edited draft as final.	Recopies final draft with no extra presentation.	Includes adequate presentation efforts with illustration, format, and style.	Impressive presentation of written work with attention to format, style, illustration, and clarity.
Self-Management	Puts writing tasks off until the last minute and seldom finishes work on time.	Allows some, but often not enough, time for writing tasks.	Allows time for writing but not enough for planning, gathering information, etc.	Listens to advice about time requirements and plans accordingly.
Language Resources	Seldom refers to language resources such as word walls or dictionaries.	Asks teacher or other students for help with words.	When reminded, uses classroom resources such as word walls and dictionaries.	Makes active use of varied classroom language resources.
Writing Traits				
Audience	Displays little or no sense of audience. Does not engage audience.	Displays some sense of audience.	Writes with audience in mind throughout.	Displays a strong sense of audience. Engages audience.
Citing Sources	The writing demonstrates little commitment to the quality and significance of research and the accuracy of the written document. Frequent errors in documentation result in instances of plagiarism and do not enable the reader to check the source.	The writing demonstrates limited commitment to the quality and significance of research and the accuracy of the written document. Documentation is sometimes used to avoid plagiarism and to enable the reader to judge how believable or important a piece of information is by checking the source. Errors sometimes violate the rules of documentation.	The writing demonstrates commitment to the quality and significance of research and the accuracy of the written document. Documentation is used to avoid plagiarism and to enable the reader to judge how believable or important a piece of information is by checking the source. Minor errors do not blatantly violate the rules of documentation.	The writing demonstrates exceptionally strong commitment to the quality and significance of research and the accuracy of the written document. Documentation is used to avoid plagiarism and to enable the reader to judge how believable or important a piece of information is by checking the source.
Elaboration (supporting details and examples that develop the main idea)	Elaboration of ideas is limited to a related list with no details or examples given.	Sketchy, redundant, or general details, which may be irrelevant, are included. Support for key ideas is very uneven.	Mix of general statements and specific details/examples is included to elaborate on ideas. Support is mostly relevant but may be uneven and lack depth in places.	For each key point/idea, specific details and supporting examples with depth are given. May use compare/contrast to support.
Focus	Insufficient length to determine if writer maintains focus. Topic is unclear or wanders. Reader has to infer the topic. Extraneous material may be present.	Topic/position/direction is unclear or reader has to infer.	Topic/position is stated and direction/purpose is previewed and maintained. Mainly stays on topic.	Topic/position is clearly stated, previewed, and maintained throughout the paper. Topics and details are tied together with a central theme or purpose that is maintained/threaded throughout the paper.

	1 Point	2 Points	3 Points	4 points
Ideas/Content	Superficial and/or minimal content is included.	The reader can understand the main ideas although they may be overly broad or simplistic, and the results may not be effective. Supporting detail is limited, insubstantial, overly general, or off topic.	The writing is clear and focused. The reader can easily understand the main ideas. Support is present, although it may be limited or rather general.	Writing is exceptionally clear, focused, and interesting. Main ideas stand out and are developed by strong support and rich details.
Organization	The writing lacks coherence; organization seems haphazard and disjointed. Plan is not evident. Facts are presented randomly with no transitions. Includes weak beginning and abrupt ending. Demonstrated no attention to paragraph organization.	An attempt has been made to organize the writing; however, the overall structure is inconsistent or skeletal. Plan is evident but loosely structured or overuses a particular pattern. Writing may be a listing of facts/ideas. Includes a weak beginning or conclusion and awkward transitions. Some paragraph organization is evident.	Organization is clear and coherent. Order and structure are present, but may seem formulaic. Plan is evident. Reasons for order of key concepts may be unclear. Beginning or conclusion is included but may lack impact. Transitions are present. Paragraph use is appropriate.	The organization enhances the central idea and its development. The order and structure are compelling and move the reader through the text easily. Plan is evident. Key concepts are logically sequenced. Beginning grabs attention. Conclusion adds impact. Uses a variety of transitions that enhance meaning. Uses paragraphs appropriately.
Sentence Fluency	The writing is difficult to follow, either choppy or rambling. Sentences are incomplete or awkward constructions force the reader to slow down or reread.	The writing tends to be mechanical rather than fluid. Occasional awkward constructions may force the reader to slow down.	The writing flows, however connections between phrases or sentences may be less than fluid. Sentence patterns are somewhat varied, contributing to ease in oral reading.	The writing has an effective flow and rhythm. Sentences show a high degree of craftsmanship, with consistently strong and varied structure that makes expressive oral reading easy and enjoyable.
Voice	The writing provides little sense of involvement or commitment. There is no evidence that the writer has chosen a suitable voice and does not engage audience.	The writer's commitment to the topic seems inconsistent. A sense of the writer may emerge at times; however, the voice is either inappropriately personal or inappropriately impersonal.	A voice is present. The writer demonstrates commitment to the topic. In places, the writing is expressive, engaging, or sincere.	The writer has chosen a voice appropriate for the topic, purpose, and audience. A unique style comes through. The writing is expressive, engaging, or sincere. A strong commitment to the topic is evident.
Word Choice	Exhibits less than minimal word usage. The writing shows an extremely limited vocabulary and frequent misuse of words. Language is monotonous. Includes no interesting words. Words and expressions are simple and may be repetitive, inappropriate, or overused.	Exhibits minimal word usage. Language is ordinary, lacking interest, precision, and variety. May be inappropriate to audience and purpose in places. The writing is filled with familiar words and phrases. Contains only a few interesting words. Words and expressions are clear, but usually more general than specific.	Exhibits adequate word usage. Words and expressions are clear and precise. Words effectively convey the intended message. The writer employs a variety of words that are functional and appropriate to audience and purpose. Contains some interesting words. Includes some vivid descriptive language.	Exhibits exceptional word usage. Words convey the intended message in an exceptionally interesting, precise, and natural way appropriate to audience and purpose. The writer employs a rich, broad range of words, which have been carefully chosen, and thoughtfully placed for impact. Frequently contains interesting words. Uses literary devices effectively.

Analytical Scoring Rubric

Name ______________________________ Date __________

Teacher ______________________________ Grade __________

	Low				High
Focuses on the topic	0	1	2	3	4
Includes appropriate level of detail	0	1	2	3	4
Has a beginning, middle, and end	0	1	2	3	4
Uses a variety of sentence types	0	1	2	3	4
Exhibits appropriate word choice and variety	0	1	2	3	4
Is written clearly	0	1	2	3	4
Uses complete sentences	0	1	2	3	4
Shows subject-verb agreement	0	1	2	3	4
Contains standard English language usage	0	1	2	3	4
Has correct punctuation	0	1	2	3	4
Has correct capitalization	0	1	2	3	4
Has correct spelling	0	1	2	3	4
Is legible	0	1	2	3	4
Overall Rating	**0**	**1**	**2**	**3**	**4**

Teacher's Notes:

____

____

____

Alternative Assessment

Different types of assessment provide multiple measures of student performance and development.

School Portfolio A school portfolio can show a student's progress from year to year. If students do a similar assignment in each grade level, the progress can be demonstrated across many years. The writing rubrics can be used to evaluate the school portfolio.

Unit Portfolio A unit portfolio can show all of the work a student has done in a certain period of time. The student can choose his or her best work to publish, display, or present to parents. The writing rubrics can be applied to evaluate the unit portfolio.

On-Demand Writing Prompt Periodically, a short, structured, and limited writing prompt that students respond to can provide valuable insight into a student's understanding of genre, conventions, or structures of writing.

Questions Teachers Ask

Questions Teachers Ask about the Developmental Nature of Writing

Q. ***Writing is fine for children once they have learned how to read, but my children are too young for this or don't come with enough early literacy experiences to write. What's expected from young children?***

A. Writing is a process, and teachers need to understand that their expectations should be different for children at different times. For some young children, just picking up a crayon and making marks on a page may be sufficient. For others, drawing a picture and talking about it is a natural part of developing understanding. Invented spelling is also natural, and teachers and parents should be encouraged rather than discouraged by these early attempts to tie oral language to writing. Children discover by doing. Early experimentation with writing is an important part of this process.

Seminar supports reluctant writers as they hear and discuss the work of other students, their ideas for topics, and their writing problems.

Q. ***How does this developmental approach work with reluctant writers?***

A. There are many reasons children are reluctant to write. Many children, even the youngest, come to school thinking that the teacher expects everything to be perfect, and if it's not, then it's wrong. Many children are reluctant to write for fear of misspelling words or of making other mistakes. Others lack confidence or are afraid their stories will be compared to those of others. Teachers need to create classrooms that encourage all children to write. Sloppy copies are welcomed, and spelling and grammar are put into proper perspective as part of editing. Each writer's work is not compared to that of others. Seminar supports reluctant writers as they hear and discuss the work of other students, their ideas for topics, and their writing problems. Group support, in addition to teacher support, is an important function in Seminar.

Questions Teachers Ask about Planning, Revising, Editing, and Publishing

Q. ***Is brainstorming with the class in order to find a single topic a good idea?***

A. While this is an often-used technique, teachers need to ask themselves "Is this what real authors do?" Authors have ownership of their topics and write about what they know or care about or what interests them. Be careful that students don't misinterpret brainstorming and think, "I must write on this topic (which I know nothing about or does not interest me)," "I must use all these words (which makes it contrived)," or "I'm going to be compared to everyone else in the class (Ugh!)."

Q. ***Is it ever OK for all students to write on the same topic?***

A. Sometimes the class itself may elect to write on a topic or use the same form. Children love to make books of riddles or write different stories that will go into a class newspaper or anthology. Sometimes children may choose to write about a particular theme or trip they've taken. Let the authors decide.

Q. ***Do students need to revise everything?***

A. No, only those drafts on which students continue to work. By taking this approach, students are encouraged to make decisions about their work and to prioritize it.

Q. ***My students read their pieces and don't see the need to revise. Everything looks fine to them. How do I get them to see where and how to change their work?***

A. Students often don't understand or value the idea of revising. Revising can be introduced naturally through writing conferences and Seminar. Students will need gentle reminders about revising, particularly in the beginning. Posting revising activities that students can use to guide them is helpful. Also, a revising checklist can be put on a chart and made available in the Writing Area or copied into each student's writing journal or Writing Folder. Start small and encourage students to take responsibility for one or two types of revising techniques, building upon that foundation during the year. Encourage authors to read their work in progress aloud or have a partner read it aloud. This type of activity sometimes makes it easier to identify parts that don't make sense, that need additional information, or that could be deleted. Remind students that revising is just as important as any of the stages in the whole writing process.

Q. ***Does every piece need to be edited?***

A. No, only those pieces that are going to be published or shared publicly in some way.

Q. ***Do students have to publish everything?***

A. Absolutely not. Not everything is worthy of publication, and authors need to be selective. Based upon feedback from Seminar, they can choose their personal favorite, a particularly creative piece, and so on.

Q. ***What do you do about children who never publish?***

A. Structure the environment to ensure that all students publish. It is perfectly acceptable to tell students that six or seven published pieces are expected a year. They can choose which pieces or get advice from their teacher or from peers. It makes sense to spread out publishing over the year. In upper grades, teachers may want to be more specific and set guidelines, for example, that student publishing should include a biography, a descriptive piece, a newspaper article, and so on. This gives students choices within limits.

Q. ***Publishing takes a lot of time. How can I get it done?***

A. Publishing can be simple; it doesn't need to be time consuming. If possible, parents, aides, and peers can help put the final copy on the computer for a more polished-looking product. Several cautions need to be kept in mind. The author and the adult need to sit down first and discuss where the illustrations will be going and what copy needs to be on that page. Second, the adult needs to remember not to change words in the story to make it sound better. Finally, even these typed copies need to be proofread to catch mistakes that may have been made during keyboarding.

Questions Teachers Ask about Managing Writing in the Classroom

Q. ***I have a small room. How can I find the space for all this?***

A. These centers do not need to be elaborate. Use shelves of bookcases for supplies and a small table for the publishing area. Plastic containers that are clearly labeled help with storage.

Writing can and should be integrated into all learning, including science, math, and social studies.

Q. ***How much time do I spend each day on writing?***

A. At the beginning of kindergarten and first grade, children may draw or write for only about ten minutes, followed by a five- or ten-minute Seminar. As the year goes on, children will be able to spend more time on writing. From second grade on, about 25 minutes for writing and another ten minutes for Seminar or sharing is appropriate. While writing is considered part of the language arts block of time, it can be done at any time during the day—in the afternoon or first thing in the morning. Writing can and should be integrated into all learning, including science, math, and social studies. The important point is that students write regularly each week, preferably every day.

Q. ***What do I tell parents who are upset when they see misspellings on papers in their child's folder?***

A. First, drafts should be marked "DRAFT" by the students. A great purchase is an ink pad and stamp that says "DRAFT." Second, parents will need some explanation of the writing process. Discuss writing expectations with parents during open house and other parent meetings.

Q. ***Can you give me any suggestions about managing centers?***

A. Student helpers can be assigned to hand out writing folders during regularly scheduled writing times. Sign-up sheets are useful in the Publishing Center to help avoid a large group of eager publishers all needing to use the same materials at the same time. Some simple rules like "only five people at the center at one time" and "only whispering is allowed" may be useful here. Management techniques should not discourage students from working together and learning from each other.

Questions Teachers Ask about Managing Writing Conferences and Seminar

Q. ***How can I get to every student every day?***

A. It is not expected that teachers will work with every student every day. Work with several students each day and use peers to help. Another alternative is to have small-group conferences with students who are having similar problems. This is particularly useful during the editing stage, which comes before publishing. Remember also that Seminar is another opportunity for feedback. Once students are comfortable with Seminar, they may want to hold small-group seminars so everyone in the group has a chance to share and receive feedback.

Q. ***How long should conferences be?***

A. Conferences should be brief and cover one or two points that the student can incorporate when revising his or her work. Conferences that are too long and cover too many points often leave the student overwhelmed and confused about where to begin. Short conferences are more valuable than long ones. (For children in kindergarten and first grade, two or three minutes is more than enough. For older children, three to five minutes is a good estimate. Age and need will help teachers decide.)

Q. ***What if students haven't finished? Can they be Seminar leaders?***

A. Yes! Work in progress as well as completed pieces should be shared. Feedback during Seminar can help students as they develop ideas and revise drafts.

Q. ***How do you get Seminar participants to pay attention?***

A. Two or three students should be leaders each day, and comments from participants should not go on endlessly. Three or four good comments that leave the author with suggestions for change is enough for one time. When necessary, the teacher needs to model meaningful comments.

Q. ***How do you get reluctant participants to share during Seminar?***

A. Some children are naturally shy or insecure and don't volunteer for Seminar. Keep track so these children don't go without sharing. To help these reluctant sharers, have them do their sharing in small-group sessions that are less intimidating than being Seminar leaders in front of the whole group. Or, the teacher or another student can read the piece to the larger group. Be sure that the author sits in a chair in front with the reader. This gets the author up in front of the group in a nonthreatening situation, and additionally, the author is there to help with any illegible words and to call on participants for feedback. Or, the teacher and the student can read the piece to the whole group together. Frequently, once an alternate reader starts reading, the reluctant author will take over naturally.

Q. ***When should Seminar be held?***

A. Seminar can be held before students write so the teacher can model strategies and students can receive feedback to use during writing. However, student-initiated seminars can be held during writing as well. This arrangement gives students time to get started, time to get feedback, and the chance to return to their writing to make changes while the suggestions are fresh in their minds. Also, seminars can be held at the end of the writing period to provide feedback to authors, as well as closure to the writing process.

Questions Teachers Ask about Evaluation

Q. ***Should students have everything correct in order to get an "A"?***

A. Students, particularly younger students, cannot be expected to get everything correct. Remember, teachers should hold students responsible only for what they have learned or are developmentally ready to learn. Consequently, evaluation should be based on how students use what they know, how they are changing, and how they are beginning to use newly introduced ideas.

Q. ***I need to give writing grades. My school requires it, and the parents want them. What do I do?***

A. Grades should be based on each student's growth and improvements that the student made during the semester. For example, teachers would point out to parents that their child is now able to revise at the word level, something he or she was unable to do previously. Grades also can be based on how successfully students have met the goals set at the end of the previous semester or marking period.

To educate parents who are used to a more traditional grading system, consider a presentation about evaluating writing at an open house at the beginning of the school year. Teachers can describe their alternative approach, explain the benefits, and show parents what to expect.

Conclusion

Let the Writers Speak for Themselves

> ***"It feels good to look at a good story and say 'I did that.'"***
>
> **Tessa Barber, Grade 5**

Students become full-fledged members of the community of writers when they take ownership of their writing; when they recognize that writing is learning, a way of organizing and reorganizing information; and when they appreciate that writing is a special way of touching those around them. Some members of ***Open Court's*** community of writers have shared their thoughts about writing. Here are their "unedited" reflections on writing.

"I like writing because you can keep it forever."
Heather Weneck, Grade 3

"Writing is fun because you get to create things. You don't have to be a pro to write."
Rachel Simmons, Grade 4

"I fL hBe wn Irit."
(I feel happy when I write.)
Deanna Steyer, Grade 1

"What makes you a better writer? Lots of quiet for me."
Malynda Schumaker, Grade 2

References

Bereiter, C. and Scardamalia, M. (1987). The *Psychology of Written Composition.* Hillsdale, NJ: Lawrence Erlbaum Associates, Inc.

Hillocks, G. (1986). *Research on Written Composition.* Urbana, IL: National Conference on Research in English.

Spandel, V. and Stiggins, R. J. (1997). *Creating Writers: Linking Writing Assessment and Instruction.* White Plains, NY: Longman Publishers.

Temple, C., Nathan, R., Temple, F., and Burris, N.A. (1993). *The Beginnings of Writing.* Needham Heights, MA: Allyn and Bacon.

Williams, J. D. (1998). *Preparing to Teach Writing.* Mahwah, New Jersey: Lawrence Erlbaum Associates, Inc.